DEDICATED TO SERVE

EMMA
M.
PHILLIPS

DEDICATED

TO

SERVE

Biographies of 31 Women of the Restoration

HERALD HOUSE
Independence
Missouri

Dedicated to my sister
Thelma May Greene

FOREWORD

A sequel to *33 Women of the Restoration,* this book contains biographical sketches of thirty-one women whose lives have influenced the church since the days of its inception in upstate New York to the present time. Each has made a unique contribution: protecting the Book of Mormon plates, being the first freed slave to unite with the church in the South, providing quarters for the original conference of the Reorganization, helping establish a frontier mission, organizing a women's aid group, teaching, translating, writing, singing. In some cases these dynamic women were directly responsible for motivating their husbands to serve the church. Often life for them was difficult—particularly when they were left at home to tend the farm or family business while their men went out to preach the gospel or minister in a leadership role. Always they did it willingly.

Whatever the service or sacrifice, whatever the era, all of these women had one thing in common—a faith that demanded their best effort. They had no calls, nor ordinations, but their ministry touched many people. Because of them lives were changed not only in their generation but in succeeding ones. The church has been—and continues to be—blessed because they were "dedicated to serve."

Paul A. Wellington
Book Editor

CONTENTS

"As women of the Restoration, we pray that we will strive more diligently to build eternal qualities into our lives. We desire to love more, and to give more of our talents. We pray that we shall continue to strive for eternal life, not only for ourselves but for those thirsting for light."

—From a prayer by Rosamond (Mrs. W. Wallace) Smith

KATHARINE

SALISBURY

Katharine* Smith and her older sister, Sophronia, became suddenly alert when they heard a loud noise and commotion outside their house. The two teen-age girls were afraid, and they had good reason to be. Someone was trying to steal the ancient records on which was engraved the history of people who had lived in America hundreds of years before.

Answering a knock at the door, Katharine found her

*In early church history, she is identified as Catherine or Catharine. In later life, letters to the *Herald* are signed "Katharine."

11

brother, Joseph Smith, Jr. Out of breath and hair fanned from running, he thrust a cloth-covered parcel into her arms. "Hide this," he said emphatically, then dashed out into the night again.

Katharine closed the door behind him. She heard people running past the house in pursuit of her brother. Although they were chasing Joseph now, she knew they might return to the house to look for the plates.

Hurrying back to the bedroom she pulled back the bed covers and placed the heavy bundle in the bed. Then she and Sophronia got into bed and pulled the covers over themselves and the plates. They heard someone enter the house, search a while, and then leave. God had permitted them to protect the Book of Mormon plates.

In the family of Joseph Smith, Sr., and Lucy Mack Smith were six sons—Alvin, Hyrum, Joseph, Samuel, Ephraim (who lived only a few days), William, and Don Carlos. Of these boys, Don Carlos was the only one younger than Katharine.

There were three daughters: Sophronia (born May 18, 1803), Katharine (born July 28, 1813), and Lucy (born July 18, 1821).

The sisters were baptized in June 1830, just two months after the organization of the church. Katharine was baptized by David Whitmer. Members of the family had a deep love for one another and spent many evenings together in the home. It was in such gatherings that the children learned to respect the Bible and to live by its teachings.

When Katharine's parents moved with other Saints to

Kirtland, Ohio, she and Lucy accompanied them. Sophronia and her husband, Calvin Stoddard, also moved to Ohio. In Kirtland Katharine and Wilkins J. Salisbury, a member of the church who was an attorney, were married on June 8, 1831, by Sidney Rigdon in the Stoddard home.

Katharine and Sophronia were among the young church women of Kirtland who made clothing for the men who built the House of the Lord. They held meetings at certain locations where looms had been set up for weaving. There were also organized groups of women who did wool carding, spinning, and knitting.

In Kirtland Wilkins followed the trade of a blacksmith instead of law. He repaired the wagons that were used to haul stone from the quarries to the building site of the temple.

Early in 1838 many of the members living in Kirtland moved to Far West, Missouri. Katharine and Wilkins and their two children, Lucy and Solomon, were in one group. Accompanying them were Sophronia Stoddard and her daughter (Calvin died in 1836), Joseph, Sr., and his wife Lucy Smith, daughter Lucy, and Don Carlos and his family. The Salisburys made the trip from Ohio to Missouri in a covered wagon. Just after they had crossed into Missouri on June 7, 1838, Katharine gave birth to a son whom they named Alvin.

The Saints were forced during the winter of 1838-39 to leave Far West. Emma Smith and her four children left early in the fall. Her husband, Joseph Smith, Jr., was in prison at Liberty, Missouri, at the time.

Traveling in one wagon were the senior Smiths, Sophronia McCleary (she was remarried in Far West),

Lucy Smith, and the Salisburys and their three children. When they reached the Mississippi River, they were met by Samuel who had left Far West earlier. He hired a ferryman to take them to Quincy on the other side of the river. His family and the William Smiths were living in the village of Plymouth, Illinois. He secured housing there for the rest of the family, and Wilkins obtained work as a blacksmith.

In the spring of 1839 many of the Saints moved from Quincy and other villages to Nauvoo, Illinois. Among those who moved to Nauvoo were Joseph and Emma Smith, Jr., their sons—Joseph, Frederick, and Alexander—and their adopted daughter, Julia.

Because Plymouth was about thirty-five miles from Nauvoo, and because travel was slow and difficult, Katharine and Wilkins were not able to take part in many of the church activities. They did, however, keep in touch with the church by reading *Times and Seasons,* a periodical printed in Nauvoo.

Even though she did not live close to them, Katharine kept track of the other members of her family. On June 4, 1840, her sister Lucy was married to Arthur Milliken, a young church elder. Nine days later a son, Don Carlos, was born to Joseph and Emma. When Father Smith became very ill, Arthur Milliken rode horseback to Plymouth to get Katharine. Before she could reach the home of her parents, her father died (September 14, 1840).

In August of the following year Katharine again made the journey to Nauvoo, this time to attend the funeral of her brother, Don Carlos. The next month a son was born to her; he was named Don Carlos. That same month the infant son (Don Carlos) of Joseph and Emma

14

Smith died, and Hyrum, the son of Hyrum Smith, died.

Katharine and Wilkins continued to live in Plymouth, Illinois, visiting Nauvoo whenever possible. On the morning of June 28, 1844, a messenger came to the Salisbury home to tell of the assassination of Joseph and Hyrum in the jail at Carthage, Illinois. Because her husband was away on business, Katharine left her children with friends and went to Nauvoo. There was now a new baby girl (born March 25, 1844) in the family; she was named Emma in honor of her aunt. Katharine remained a few days in Nauvoo with the widows of her brothers and with her aged mother, then returned to her own family.

There was unrest in Nauvoo and in the small nearby communities where church members lived. Saints were afraid more mobs would form. Those who were not members of the church were afraid the Saints would retaliate because of the murders. On several occasions the Salisburys found messages tacked to their house door telling them to leave or be killed. During the summer of 1844 they moved to Beardstown, Illinois, in hopes they would be safer. Wilkins started a blacksmith shop, but people would not bring their business to him because his wife was a sister of "Ol' Joe, the Mormon."

A month after the murder of her two brothers, another brother, Samuel, died as a result of abuse by the mob. Five months later (November 17, 1844) a son was born to Emma Smith; she named him David.

Because the Salisburys believed their family would be safer in Nauvoo than in Beardstown, they moved there in the summer of 1845, traveling at night on back roads

15

to avoid being seen. In Nauvoo, another son, Lorain, was born to them.

In the spring of 1846 many of the church people went with Brigham Young. Katharine sorrowed as the wives of her brothers Hyrum and Samuel and their children joined this group. Emma Smith refused to leave Nauvoo, and she and Katharine remained good friends.

In the spring of 1846 the Salisburys bought a raft, loaded on it their possessions (including a cow), and started to float down the Mississippi toward St. Louis. With them were their six children: Lucy, Solomon, Alvin, Don Carlos, Emma, and Lorain. As the raft rounded a bend in the river, it was struck by a steamboat and wrecked. All members of the family managed to make the safety of the shore near Alexandria, Missouri, but their possessions were lost. The cow reached shore also, but in the confusion someone stole it.

They lived in Alexandria until the following year. Here their daughter Emma died and was buried. They next moved to Macedonia. Church members had established this village in 1840, calling it Ramus. Later the name was changed to Macedonia, and still later to Webster. When the Saints moved away from Nauvoo, they had also moved away from this village, leaving several houses empty. People of the neighborhood had taken all tools and furniture left behind in the houses and barns. With limited equipment Wilkins opened a blacksmith shop.

Another child, Frederick, was born to them in 1850. Three years later—on October 28, 1853—Wilkins died of typhoid fever. Katharine and her children continued to live in Webster. Years later a grandson, Herbert Salisbury, wrote: "She was given a sum of money by someone in Utah so she could move her family to Utah. Instead she bought forty acres in Illinois and built a house, and made her home there until she died."

On May 8, 1855, Katharine's mother, Lucy Smith, died in Nauvoo. On her way to attend the funeral Sophronia, Katharine's older sister, stopped at Webster to visit the Salisbury home. During their visit, the two sisters recalled how they had protected the plates of the Book of Mormon when they had been young girls.

On May 3, 1857, Katharine married Joseph Younger who lived at Fountain Green, Illinois.

During the period of reorganization (1852-1860) Katharine must have heard of what was happening in Wisconsin in the Wildermuth and Powers homes. Because she and Emma Smith remained friends throughout the years, Emma no doubt told her of the two young men coming from Wisconsin in 1856 to ask Joseph Smith III to serve as president of the church.

Katharine's oldest son, Solomon, was one of the people instrumental in starting the Pilot Grove, Illinois, branch on July 13, 1873. He also served as pastor. That same year Katharine united with the Reorganization. All of her children became members of the church. When Emma Smith died in Nauvoo in 1879, Katharine's four sons—Solomon, Alvin, Don Carlos, and Frederick—served as pallbearers.

When she was called to make a public statement defending the Book of Mormon, Katharine gladly did so. The affidavit bore the date of April 15, 1881. In 1899 a pamphlet was published by a faction of

17

Mormonism in which the statement was made that Brother and Sister Salisbury, William Smith, Lucy Smith Milliken, and others had signed a paper saying they believed that J. J. Strang was to be the church president. Katharine wrote a letter for the newspapers in which she said, "My mother was present when young Joseph Smith was ordained and set apart by his father to lead the church before his father was taken to Carthage and killed. That is why we never followed any leader, for we all knew who the right leader was."

She died February 2, 1900, at the home of her son Frederick in Hancock County, Illinois. Elder James McKiernan, prominent church missionary, conducted the funeral service. She is buried beside Wilkins Salisbury.

A descendant, Warren L. Van Dine, writes, "She is buried at Webster, Illinois, in a rural cemetery located about thirty miles east and a little south of Nauvoo."

CAROLINE

BOOKER

Caroline pressed her small daughter to her. Almost three years old! Would this child be taken from her as her son had been? She could still feel the agony of having her firstborn pulled from her arms by the slave trader and taken away to be sold. Where was that son? Caroline would never know what became of him.

A small finger traced a tear as it trickled down the weeping woman's black cheek. "Mama sick?" the little girl asked in childish sympathy.

Caroline smiled down at her daughter, Caroline. "Mama is fine," she lied. How could a mother be anything but sick in her soul at the fear that her three-year-old daughter would be sold into slavery? It was the policy in several southern states for slave traders to take Negro children when they were only a few years old and sell them as companions for white children. They would grow up together, but the Negro children were constantly in subjection to the white ones.

Caroline's husband, Benjamin, was a slave on the same plantation that was owned by a man named William Booker. Caroline had been born in Monroe County, Alabama, in 1834. Her mother-in-law, Lucy, was also a slave on the Booker plantation. Lucy knew stories about the earlier days of slavery. When the two women were together in their humble home, Lucy would tell of how white slave traders would anchor their ships off the coast of Africa. Then they would sneak into the communities and steal boys and girls. These kidnapped Negro children were forced to remain in the dark, damp lower part of the sailing vessels during the weeks required to cross the ocean to the United States. Those who were still alive when they reached their destination were branded and sold into slavery. Those who were dead or very sick were thrown into the ocean.

The Civil War began in April of 1861. Slavery was one of the points of contention between the northern states and the southern states. Frequently whispered reports came to Caroline and Benjamin that battles were being fought, and that slaves were escaping and making their way into Canada. Some, of course, were caught and punished.

Early in the spring of 1863 came a message that brought joy to Caroline. The slaves had been given their freedom. Little Caroline, born in 1860, would never be sold as her brother had been. On January 1, 1863,

President Abraham Lincoln signed the Emancipation Proclamation that gave freedom to over 3,000,000 enslaved Negroes.

Several southern states had a law declaring that slaves could never be given freedom. Consequently, some of the white owners paid no attention to the Emancipation Proclamation. At the Battle of Gettysburg in July 1863 over 20,000 Confederate soldiers were killed, and southerners began to realize that they might lose the war.

Back in Nauvoo, Illinois, Joseph Smith III was declaring that he would do what he could to overcome slavery. He said, "We believed that this was to be a land devoted to religious and civil liberty for all races of men alike, and that the fulfillment of divine decree was imminent, even if by bloodshed."

Southern Negroes moved into northern communities and joined the northern army. Although white people wanted the Negroes to be free, many did not want Negroes to live in their communities or to be employed at equal pay. In July 1863 in New York City, over 2,000 people were killed in racial uprisings.

Benjamin and Caroline continued to live on the Booker plantation. Another son, Perry, was born to them on May 14, 1864. The year 1865 was important to them for several reasons. They rejoiced when they heard that the southern armies had surrendered; but they sorrowed when they learned that President Lincoln had been assassinated. On December 18, 1865, the government passed the thirteenth amendment declaring that there would be no more slavery in the United States or any land belonging to it.

At a world conference of the church held in October 1865 at Council Bluffs, Iowa, it was decided that missionaries should be sent into the southern states. Many people of the South were opposed to the church because of the firm stand it took against slavery. Work on the plantations could not be done because the slaves had left. White southern leaders were urging them to return to their previous locations and take care of the crops.

The fact that Benjamin, Caroline, their children, and Lucy remained on the plantation indicates that William Booker was kinder than some other masters. During the slave period, Negroes had only first names. Now they could have last names; they could create their own or take the name of someone they honored. Benjamin and Caroline took the name of Booker. They were now paid for their services and could leave the plantation if they desired. Other children were born to them.

William Booker permitted missionaries to hold services in his home, and he and his wife Martha invited neighbors to come hear them. On March 6, 1866, the first congregation of the church in Alabama was organized in their home; it was called the Lone Star Branch. As Caroline worked about the house she heard much about the church, and she saw her former slave master change into a true Christian.

Caroline wanted to become a member of the Reorganized Church of Jesus Christ of Latter Day Saints. When she mentioned this to Benjamin, he said firmly, "No, Caroline. We have our freedom. Do not push this too far. If you mention this to the white folk in the big house they will say you cannot be one of them."

Caroline argued that she believed the church represented Jesus Christ and that when the gospel was restored to earth it was for all people. Benjamin and Lucy tried to impress on her that Negroes would not be welcome in this church. The discussion continued day after day, and prayers were said. Finally Benjamin said to Caroline, "Go ahead. Ask if you can join the church with the restored gospel. And if you can, I will also."

On July 13, 1868, eight Negroes became members of the Lone Star Branch. The first baptized was Caroline Booker. Both she and her husband were baptized by G. R. Scogin. Later—on October 6, 1868—Lucy Booker was baptized by her former slave master, William Booker, now an elder in the church.

It was difficult for members of the Lone Star Branch because their white neighbors shunned them for permitting former slaves to be equal to them in the church. Other Negroes tormented Benjamin, Caroline, and the others for joining the church and called them "white folks' niggers." But Caroline clung to her beliefs and taught them to her children. When Perry was ten years old he stood up and bore testimony that he wanted to serve God. He had been baptized June 1, 1873.

In 1881 Benjamin Booker moved his family from the plantation to St. Joseph, Alabama, where another branch of the church was located. Members of the Lone Star Branch gave them letters of recommendation saying they were Saints in good standing. Lucy Booker also moved with them.

Now Caroline was in a home of her own. Like other mothers she did all she could to see that her children received an education and that they learned to read the

Bible. Benjamin Booker did construction work and various types of manual labor to support his family. He and Caroline planted a garden which their five sons and three daughters helped to tend. When grown, Perry became pastor of the St. Joseph Branch which in 1887 had a membership of twenty-five. Other Booker sons were called to the priesthood also.

Although the St. Joseph Branch grew slowly, the Lone Star Branch declined. For a while it was disorganized because there were no officers to take charge of it.

In the fall of 1889 Lucy Booker died; she was over eighty at the time of her death. Her daughter Caroline gave her loving care in her declining years. Benjamin was also becoming feeble. Some of their children married and moved to Florida. Caroline, Benjamin, and their families settled in Chumuckla, a small community about fifty miles from Pensacola, Florida.

After Benjamin died in May of 1901 Caroline went to live with her daughter, Mrs. Alice Wiggins; she died in May of 1915 and is buried in Chumuckla, Florida.

Today the descendants of Benjamin and Caroline Booker and those of William and Martha Booker serve side by side in the priesthood, in the department of women, and in community work. Elder William Blue, a descendant of Benjamin and Caroline, while serving as a delegate from Pensacola District at World Conference presented a resolution concerning greater ministry to various ethnic groups. Mrs. Peggy Michael, a descendant of William and Martha Booker and also a delegate from Pensacola District, supported his resolution.

Peggy Michael writes, "The descendants of Caroline and Benjamin Booker and the descendants of William and Martha Booker dedicate themselves to the task of showing to the world a brotherhood that has grown through the gospel of Jesus Christ."

MAHALA
ROGERS

Mahala," said young Israel L. Rogers to his wife, "I don't think we should travel on to Nauvoo with the other church members. I think we should settle in this part of Illinois."

Mahala looked about her. "This land is good for farming. I would like to live here," she agreed.

Israel and Mahala were that way about decisions. Ever since their marriage on February 24, 1839, they had planned together.

When they had first heard the restored gospel a few years after their marriage, they had thoughtfully discussed it. Israel united with the church while they were

26

still living in New York. Later they settled on a farm near what eventually became Sandwich, Illinois.

Mahala Salisbury was born August 17, 1817, in Chenango County, New York. Although Illinois differed from her native state she loved the midwest farm on which she and her husband made their home. They worked hard, and the fertile soil yielded bountifully. A large barn was built to contain the harvest. Although they had a small house at first, they later built a large home with spacious rooms.

The report in the summer of 1844 that Joseph Smith, Jr., and Hyrum Smith had been assassinated came as a shock to them. Like many other church members, they could not determine who should be the immediate leader of the church, so they remained religious people with no church connections.

When W. W. Blair and E. C. Briggs visited them in 1859 Israel treated them coolly. The men told about the Reorganization which was the continuation of the original church, and said that they had faith that Joseph Smith III would take his place as leader of the church. Although Mahala's husband would not listen to them, she was favorably impressed.

She talked with her husband, and prayed with him. Eventually he said, "I will consider the Reorganization, but I doubt if Young Joseph will ever become the leader, and I doubt if I ever unite with the movement."

Both Mahala and Israel attended the special conference held in Amboy, Illinois, in June of 1859, and she was baptized into the Reorganized Church on June 12, 1859.

The semiannual conference was held October 6-10,

1859, in the large grain barn on the Rogers farm. All the food for the Saints was furnished by the Rogers family. Women attending the conference slept in the house, while the men slept in the haymow of the barn.

One of the first branches of the Reorganization (Fox River) was organized November 18, 1859, in the Rogers home. Mahala was a charter member. Numerous meetings of the branch were later held in the home.

Mahala never forgot the events of the following March when her husband and W. W. Blair and William Marks went by train to Nauvoo to visit Joseph Smith III. They brought back the news that he had promised to attend the April 1860 conference to be held at Amboy, Illinois. It was at that conference that he agreed to take his place as prophet of the church. Israel was made presiding bishop.

Mahala was busy during May of 1865, for that month the leading men of the church held a council in the Rogers home. The revelation through Joseph Smith III received by these men became Section 116 in the Doctrine and Covenants.

A significant wedding was performed November 12, 1869, in the Rogers home. It must have pleased Mahala that President Joseph Smith III and Bertha Madison would travel from Nauvoo to her home to be married.

Bishop Rogers was always generous in lending the church money. At the time of the April 1870 General Conference the church owed him over $4,000. At that time a large number of members found it difficult to recognize the importance of paying tithing. Bishop Rogers said that instead of his being repaid this large sum of money, it should be considered his tithe. Mahala was pleased to have her husband mark this "in its proper place on the tithe books." She knew it would encourage others to pay their tithes. Four thousand dollars was a large sum of money in view of the fact that at the end of the conference the church had only $43.76 to its credit.

Mahala and Israel Rogers were the parents of six children, two boys and four girls. As they grew older they found the heavy farm work difficult and moved into a house in Sandwich. (One of their sons continued to live on the farm.) They bought a church building and moved it into Sandwich; members of the Fox River Branch attended services here.

Mahala died at home on September 22, 1892. She is buried in a cemetery only a few miles from Sandwich.

She was a woman of outstanding insight and great faith. Because of her influence, her husband recognized the Reorganized Church. All during the years in which he gave guidance to the church as bishop, she worked faithfully at his side.

ANN
WILDERMUTH

A nn Wildermuth looked out the window of her pioneer home toward the new grave in the orchard. It was small, for it was the grave of her year-old son. As she stood looking she recalled the events that had happened since the Wildermuth family had moved to Wisconsin.

Born March 3, 1814, in Ohio, she grew to womanhood there and on November 15, 1831, was married to David Wildermuth. In the spring of 1846 they journeyed to Yellowstone, Wisconsin, to establish a home. Ann's brother Cyrus Newkirk, and his family had moved to Wisconsin in 1843 and had written letters urging the Wildermuths to join them. Ann loved her pioneer home in Wisconsin. David made a living by working on their farm and in the local lead mines. The few families in Yellowstone and the neighboring village of Blanchardville were friendly.

The Wildermuths attended a Protestant church. At least they did until David and the pastor had a dispute over whether the local church's organization resembled the organization of the church in the New Testament. David Wildermuth contended that no church on earth was organized in the same way. After that the minister "withdrew the hand of fellowship" from the Wildermuth family.

Then came the sudden death of their small son. Because they were no longer attending the local church, they hesitated to ask the pastor to conduct the funeral service. Two of their neighbors, Mr. and Mrs. Fretwell, were in the house when the child died. Mr. Fretwell explained that they had a missionary from their church staying at their home for a few days, and that he would be willing to conduct the funeral service. Mrs. Fretwell consoled Ann Wildermuth. "Elder Zenos Gurley is a good, kind man. I am sure he will help you." And then she explained, "Several years ago we were members of the Church of Jesus Christ of Latter Day Saints that had headquarters in Nauvoo, Illinois. Elder Gurley was a missionary then."

Sympathetic neighbors and friends came to the funeral. After the service Elder Gurley remained in the Wildermuth home to comfort Ann and David. He told them about the Book of Mormon, Kirtland, Independence, and Nauvoo. He also told them that many of the church members had fled to the unexplored lands that

31

were west of the boundary of the United States. "At the present time," he told his new friends, "I am a follower of James J. Strang, but I cannot truthfully say I believe in his doctrine. It is different from the old church. The original church was like sweet water. This church is like bitter water. Bitter and sweet water cannot come from the same fountain."

During the following weeks, Elder Gurley held a series of meetings in the Wildermuth house. Neighbors came to attend. Although this meant extra work for Ann, she appreciated the opportunity for her family to learn about the restored gospel.

In August of 1850 Ann, David, and three of their children were baptized in the Yellowstone River by Elder Gurley and became members of the church led by J. J. Strang. After the service Ann's brother Cyrus told the Wildermuths, "Because you have joined the Mormons our families can no longer be friends."

At a church service in 1850 the Yellowstone Branch was organized with about twenty-four members. Elder Gurley became the pastor. David Wildermuth was ordained an elder and became his assistant. Edwin Wildermuth, a son, was ordained a priest. Ann, who had a fine soprano voice, led the singing and frequently sang solos for services.

Eventually the Newkirks became interested in the restored gospel, left their church, and joined the Yellowstone Branch.

In the fall of 1851 Brother Gurley heard a heavenly voice: "Rise up, cast off all that claim to be prophets, and go forth and preach the gospel and say that God will raise up a prophet to complete his work." At first he and others did not understand the words "Cast off all that claim to be prophets." Then they heard that J. J. Strang, their leader, was teaching polygamy as were the leaders in Utah.

Members of the Yellowstone Branch "cast off" the leadership of J. J. Strang. They were a group by themselves, waiting for the time when there would be a reorganization of the original church and a divinely appointed leader.

Then a missionary, David Powell, came from Beloit, Wisconsin, fifty miles away, with a special message from the pastor, Jason W. Briggs. Powell said, "We have been praying for guidance in our branch just as you have been praying here. Brother Briggs has received a revelation. I have brought a copy of it."

Ann Wildermuth was thrilled as she read the revelation, for it declared that a son of Joseph Smith, Jr., would become the leader of the church. During those trying days she did the best she could to teach her children about the restored gospel.

Gurley, however, felt that he must have assurance before accepting the revelation from Beloit. He and others continued to pray. At a meeting of a few of the Yellowstone Branch members, God spoke again: "The successor of Joseph Smith is Joseph Smith, the son of Joseph Smith the Prophet. It is his right by lineage, saith the Lord, your God." After this event Elder Gurley sent this message to Jason W. Briggs; "We have received evidence of your revelation."

Ann knew that Joseph Smith III was living in Nauvoo with his mother and stepfather, and that he had not united with any of the factions of Mormonism. He was a respected citizen, living peacefully among his neighbors.

A preliminary conference was held June 12, 1852, near Beloit. Zenos Gurley, Jason Briggs, and others united their efforts to reorganize the church. A general conference was held the following year at Blanchardville, at which the reorganization was effected. Among the first apostles was Reuben Newkirk, Ann's nephew. Two of her sons, Edwin and Eli, were ordained to the office of seventy. Ann was thankful she had taken time to teach them about Christ's church.

The Wildermuths moved in 1856 to Willow Township, Wisconsin, about eighty miles from Yellowstone. Here they cleared land and built a house. Willow Branch was organized October 12, 1863, in their home. Ann was pleased that two branches had been organized in their home.

During the Civil War, three of her sons fought on the northern side. Edwin returned home safely; John and Henry died and were buried in the southern part of the United States.

On a cold fall morning in 1856 Samuel H. Gurley (son of Zenos) and Edmund C. Briggs (brother of Jason) left their homes in Wisconsin to travel to Nauvoo to ask Joseph Smith III if he would become leader of the Reorganization or if they should look for another. Ann and David waited patiently for these two young men to return from Nauvoo with their report, but only Gurley came back. Briggs remained in Nauvoo to do missionary work. Gurley reported, "Joseph Smith would not accept leadership. He said he was going to wait until God let him know that he should be the leader. He said he needed a power and knowledge greater than his own." To Ann, this sounded like wisdom.

In 1868 the financial depression in Wisconsin left many people without means of support. That same year lice destroyed most of the crops. Except for hard work and constant prayer, the Wildermuths might have lost their land and possessions.

Besides caring for ten children of her own, Ann took into her home five grandchildren. She remained true to the church all her life. In her old age she delighted in singing the hymns she had sung in her youth. Her husband died and was buried in the Wildermuth Cemetery in Willow, Wisconsin. Ann died January 2, 1907, and was buried beside him.

MARIA

POWERS

Born January 14, 1824, in Quebec, Maria Moulton later moved to Ontario where she was married to Samuel Powers in January of 1842. Six years later they and their children left Ontario to establish their home in Rock County, Wisconsin.

One of the first things they did when they reached the site of their new home was to plant the small fruit trees they had brought with them from Canada. During the months of travel, Maria had carefully tended these trees. As a result she and Samuel had one of the first

36

orchards in Wisconsin. Both were industrious. Maria had a sewing machine and was a capable seamstress. She also taught her daughters to design and sew their own clothes. A luxury item in the Powers household was an organ, brought over the rough, narrow roads to their pioneer home. Maria was a gifted musician and, although she had little time for it, she taught her children to appreciate music and to make it part of their daily lives.

While living in Canada Samuel and Maria had heard several sermons by Elder Jehiel Savage of the Latter Day Saint Church. They were impressed, but they did not unite with the Restoration. When they moved to Wisconsin they were members of a Protestant church. The neighborhood in which they settled was near Beloit where a small group of Saints lived. These people had followed various leaders and had become disillusioned. Jason Briggs served as their pastor. They held to the doctrine of the original church, expecting a son of Joseph Smith, Jr., to become president someday.

Maria and Samuel made friends with the Saints but did not join the church. Then Samuel became very ill and remained in a critical condition for a long time. During this period he thought deeply about the religious needs of his family. Maria had the full burden and responsibility of managing their farm and could spare little time away from it. However, when she heard how God had spoken to Zenas Gurley and Jason Briggs, she felt that as a family they should find out more about the church these men represented. Like others, they traveled by wagon to attend all-day meetings. They became convinced of the truth of the restored gospel and saw a need for it in their lives and in the lives of their children.

Maria and Samuel were baptized in 1852 by Zenas Gurley and became faithful workers in the Beloit-Newark Branch. Maria made a constant effort to tell others about the restored gospel. "I must make up for my procrastination," she would explain.

Samuel was called to the priesthood and became the pastor of the Beloit-Newark Branch. In 1854 he was ordained a seventy and in 1855 an apostle. This required his being away from home often. Maria again took over the complete care of the family and farm. To the children she would cheerfully remark, "Your father must be about his heavenly Father's business."

The April 1859 conference of the church was held at Beaverton, Illinois, about thirty miles from the Powers home; Samuel presided over the meetings. At this conference a number of people who had belonged to various factions were rebaptized; they wanted to be members of the church that was being reorganized. Elizabeth Blair, Maria's close friend, was baptized by Samuel Powers. Men and women affiliated with the original church who had drifted away during the unsettled conditions in Nauvoo now became members.

At the Amboy Conference, held in April of 1860, Apostle Powers was one of the men selected to help with the ordination of Joseph Smith III to the presidency of the world church. At this conference Maria became acquainted with Emma Smith.

Years passed. The apple trees in the orchard bore repeated crops of juicy apples. Nine children were born to Maria, but only six reached adulthood. Again Samuel Powers became sick and found it difficult to do much work. Maria continued caring for the children, sewing, planting, and cleaning. She enjoyed her talent for music as she worked and studied at every available moment.

On February 16, 1873, at the age of fifty-four, Samuel Powers died. Joseph Smith III, president of the church, wrote about him, "He was one of the best and ablest men of the church."

Soon after the death of her husband Maria moved to the village of Afton near the farm of her eldest son and his wife. Most of her children were married and in homes of their own. Only her seven-year-old twin daughters were with her. In 1880, she moved to Janesville, Wisconsin, so these daughters would have a better opportunity to receive a good education. She remained there until they were grown and married.

During all these years, she and Elizabeth Blair continued their friendship. They could not visit each other often, but they wrote long, friendly letters about their families and their church activities.

Maria Powers passed away November 21, 1901, at the home of a granddaughter, Mrs. Helen Sloan, in Cameron, Missouri. She was an invalid the last five years of her life, but this granddaughter said of her, "I never heard my grandmother say a cross word."

ELIZABETH

BLAIR

The first summer eighteen-year-old
Elizabeth Doty Blair lived on the
farm was a time of difficult adjustments. Farming was
new and strange to her, for she had always lived in a
city. Just the Christmas before (1849), she had married
William W. Blair in Dixon, Illinois. The farm on which
they were making their home had belonged to her
father.

Four years later the Blairs left the farm and moved to
East Paw Paw, a village near Amboy, Illinois, and
opened a mercantile store (William had been employed
in a store prior to their marriage). Here they joined a
religious group and remained with it until November

1856, when something happened that completely changed their lives. One evening, just before closing time, two young men—Edmund C. Briggs and Samuel Gurley—came to the store. Edmund had lived in Amboy in 1853 and the Blairs had been acquainted with him. He had come to tell William about the branch in Blanchardville, Wisconsin, and about the revelations his brother Jason had received. Gurley mentioned the Wildermuth family, Yellowstone Branch, and the revelation his father had received.

"And now," said one of the men, "we are on our way to Nauvoo, Illinois, to ask Joseph Smith III if he plans to take his place as head of the church or if we should select someone else. We are telling all members of the early church and those people who are interested in the church that the time is near at hand when the church is again to be established upon earth."

William Blair became so interested that he invited the two men home with him. "My wife will want to hear about this trip you are making," he told the young men. But Elizabeth was not happy to meet them. Years later, she explained why: "My husband was always bringing traveling ministers home for the night. I got tired of it. I told him he could just wait on these young men himself. After I got supper for them, I went to choir practice at the church I was attending." When she returned home she could hear the three men discussing religion in the parlor. She went directly to the bedroom but stood just inside the door and listened to them.

It was after midnight when William came to bed. He asked if the conversation had kept her awake. "I have been listening to those ninnies try to talk," she said. "It is the most ridiculous thing I have ever heard." She was proud of the way her husband had been able to argue his side.

As always on cold mornings, William got up first to build the fire. As Elizabeth lay in bed thinking about the events of the night before, it seemed that words appeared on the wall in front of her. She was told to consider well the message of the young men.

After getting their breakfast, she and the children attended the local church, but all during the service she thought about the young men and her husband at home. It seemed the young men could not answer his questions and could not support their point of view. She felt almost sorry for them.

When she returned home she went into the parlor where the men were. Now things were different. Her husband was not able to confound the young men. Suddenly Edmund C. Briggs stood up, took a copy of the Book of Mormon in his hand, and began to read rapidly and clearly. He read the answers to all the difficult questions that William Blair had asked. Elizabeth was amazed and a little frightened. Her husband took the book and said, "Let me read that for myself." He looked the page over carefully. "I do not see the answers you have just read."

Briggs spoke with determination. "Every word that I read was written plainly before me. You now have answers to your questions." Elizabeth and William were bewildered. God had performed a miracle in their home. They had witnessed it. Then Elder Gurley arose and spoke in prophecy, telling the Blairs many things that would happen to them in the future, including the blessing of good health. Elizabeth and one of the children had not been well for over a year. After this event they were to become strong and healthy.

During the Christmas holidays of 1856 the Blairs traveled by train and horse-drawn sleigh to visit the Saints in Wisconsin. They were pleased with what they found. The next spring William attended a conference held at Zarahemla, Wisconsin. When he returned home he told Elizabeth that he had been baptized April 7, 1857, by Elder Zenas Gurley, and the following day he had been ordained an elder. In the fall of 1858 he was ordained an apostle. It was not until April of 1859, however, that Elizabeth was baptized.

The Blairs sold their store and returned to farming. While her husband was away on preaching assignments, Elizabeth and the children took care of the farm. Among the Saints there was constant talk about Joseph Smith III's accepting leadership of the church. He said he was waiting for God to manifest what he should do.

During the winter of 1859-60 a vision was given to Elizabeth Blair in which she saw Joseph Smith III come to the platform of the impending conference and take his place as head of the church. She had never seen him in real life, but she knew him in the vision.

At a prayer meeting of church people in Zarahemla in February 1860 she stood and told about her vision. She felt sure that this eldest son of Joseph Smith, Jr., would receive and accept his call from God. As soon as she had sat down, she regretted having told about her vision. She wished she had waited to see if it really would come true. From February to April the people talked about

Elizabeth's vision, and the more they talked the more she wished she had kept her vision to herself.

Another important visitor came to the Blair home in 1860—Israel L. Rogers. He explained, "Joseph Smith III sent a letter to William Marks. He says he is considering becoming the president of the church. He wants Marks and a couple of other men to visit him before the conference at Amboy next month. Will you go with us?"

The invitation pleased Elizabeth, and she hurried to get her husband's clothes ready. This was an honor; it was also a new confirmation of her vision.

When her husband returned home a few days later he told Elizabeth that both Joseph Smith III and his mother, Emma Smith Bidamon, hoped to attend the conference. Elizabeth also made plans to attend.

The evening before the conference a prayer meeting was held at the home of Brother Stone, about a mile and a half from Amboy. Elizabeth and William Blair attended. Also attending was Joseph Smith III and Emma Smith. Later Elizabeth wrote about this meeting: "Emma Smith stood up and bore testimony to the truth of the latter-day work and the prophetic mission of her husband. She said she had known for sixteen years that her son would continue the work of his father."

The next day—April 6, 1860—Elizabeth Blair was among those people who saw Joseph Smith III ordained to the office of the president of the church. William Blair was one of the men who assisted with the ordination.

On the evening of April 8 a number of the Saints visited the Blair home. Among them were President

44

Smith and his mother. Elizabeth had the privilege of hearing Emma recall the days in old Nauvoo.

That summer Brother Blair's missionary work took him to Kirtland, Ohio. From there he wrote to Elizabeth: "The town has a sorry look, and the condition of the Temple is pitiful. Its walls inside and out, also its trimmings and decorations, are badly defaced." That summer, while William was away, their young daughter died.

Elizabeth and the three remaining children often went with Brother Blair on his missionary assignments. They traveled by wagon. Elizabeth frequently drove with them; they carried a tent and cooking equipment.*

Elizabeth was interested in the manuscript of the Inspired Version which had been preserved by Ann Scott Davis. She was pleased that her husband was selected as one of the men to go to Emma to secure the manuscript in the spring of 1866.

William served as an apostle from October 7, 1858, until April 10, 1873, when he became a member of the First Presidency. Elizabeth enjoyed showing her children their father's name in the Doctrine and Covenants.

Elizabeth was an active member of the Ladies Aid Society and held offices in that organization. She was present April 6, 1888, when the cornerstone of Stone Church was laid by Joseph Smith III and her husband.

In 1868 women were given the first opportunity to vote at a general conference of the Reorganized Church. Prior to this they could not serve as delegates and could not express opinions. The conference minutes of 1893

---

*Five sons and two daughters were eventually born to the Blairs.

record that a number of women served as delegates. Elizabeth represented Decatur District.

Brother Blair died April 18, 1896, while on his way home from a conference. He had become sick while at the conference and insisted on returning home alone by train. After his death his wife continued to live in their home in Lamoni, Iowa.

Because her health was good, Elizabeth was able to attend reunions and to visit friends in other cities. She was happy to tell people about the early days of the Reorganization and about her experience at the Amboy Conference. She was always a good student and lived by the motto: "It is not safe to move without knowledge. I will myself make inquiry."

She died June 8, 1912, at the home of a son, David, in Kansas City, Missouri, and was buried in Lamoni, Iowa.

Her husband once wrote about her, "I recognize the hand of a kind Providence in my meeting with and finally being united in marriage with her, as I am conscious that our marriage was one of the brightest and most important periods of my life."

EMMA

PILGRIM

Although the Saints were driven out of Independence, Missouri, in November 1833, a branch of the Reorganized Church was organized in the courthouse at Independence in November 1874. At this organization meeting were George and Emma Pilgrim.

Emma's dark hair and complexion revealed the fact that she was part Indian. Her parents, Brother and Sister Parson, were among the members who had been forced in 1833 to leave their homes in Independence. They had fled with others into Clay County, Missouri. It was there, near Liberty, that Emma was born on April 27,

47

1835. As a small child she was among those driven from their homes in Far West during the winter of 1838-39. On February 22, 1852, she became the wife of George W. Pilgrim.

The Independence branch of the Reorganized Church had first been organized in 1873, but because members lived quite a distance from one another and traveling was difficult, it was disorganized. Meetings and church school continued to be held in homes, however.

Emma and George had been baptized in 1874 by a missionary who came to preach in the home of their friends, Brother and Sister Albert Noble. An item in an old newspaper reports: "Brother and Sister Pilgrim were among the first people to return to Independence." Emma was the niece of a former apostle of the church, John E. Page.

The Pilgrims and their two sons, Charles and Bert, lived on a farm a few miles northeast of Independence. Nearby was the home of Brother and Sister Noble who had been the first to return. They came in the fall of 1867, but before the branch could be organized Brother Noble died (August 24, 1872).

At the 1874 organization meeting Elder George Pilgrim was made the pastor. For some time services were held in the courthouse. Then so many church members moved to Independence that the courthouse could not hold them and a hall had to be rented. Here Emma Pilgrim taught classes in the church school.

The year 1875 was a desolate one in Independence because hordes of grasshoppers destroyed gardens and crops. Not far from the Pilgrim home was an orchard of five hundred peach trees that grasshoppers stripped of leaves. That same year Elder Heman C. Smith conducted missionary services for one month; some of these meetings were held in the Pilgrim home. Emma invited her neighbors to attend.

The following year a letter from George Pilgrim was published in the *Saints' Herald*. He wrote that the crops and gardens were good. He also stated that members found it difficult to meet because of their "scattered" condition. Brother Pilgrim was still pastor in 1877 when Joseph Smith III visited the Saints in Independence.

The women of Independence organized the Sisters' Aid Society (sometimes called Ladies' Aid Society) during the winter of 1878-79 in order to earn money for the construction of a church building and to help the needy people of the city. Emma Pilgrim served as president of this organization.

The first world conference ever held in Independence convened in 1882. Meetings were conducted in a rented hall, and the local Christian Church permitted use of its font for baptismal services. The Independence newspaper published reports of the conference. Reading these, Sister Pilgrim recalled how her parents had been forced to leave Missouri, and she was thankful that conditions were now better.

There was indeed an urgent need for a church building. A lot was purchased on East Lexington Street in Independence. Brother Fred Campbell, a brick manufacturer, constructed a kiln in the center of the lot and used the clay around it for making bricks. Foundations and walls were built around the kiln. When bricks were in the drying process, Emma often assisted in covering them before a rain. Under her direction the

Sisters' Aid Society did much to decorate the interior of the church. The rostrum was covered with a deep red carpet, and the pulpit was draped with matching velvet.

When the building was dedicated July 6, 1884, there were over three hundred members. Joseph Smith III returned to Independence for the dedication. The church would hold 350 people and some members said, "Now we have a large enough church. There will never be more than 350 church members living in Independence."

In a few years the new building was too small for the growing congregation, and plans were made to build a larger edifice. Again Emma Pilgrim led the Sisters' Aid Society in earning money for erecting a church building. This was known as the "Saints' Church" but later it became known as Stone Church. For many years it was the largest building in the city.

Sorrow came to Brother and Sister Pilgrim when their son Charles died on October 28, 1891. Sister Pilgrim was so sick during the winter of 1892-93 that she was confined to her home almost constantly. When she attended church late in January, it was mentioned in *Zion's Ensign*.

Because of her failing health, 1896 was the last year she served as president of the Sisters' Aid Society. The women gave her a vote of thanks for her outstanding work when she resigned. Mrs. Mary Jane Warnky succeeded her as president.

During the winter 1905-06 George Pilgrim became ill. According to the local newspaper he was "suffering from pheumona." Emma, who was not well herself, did all she could to care for her companion during his long illness. On June 22, 1906, he died.

After his death Emma continued to live in Independence and to attend Stone Church. A year later she died in her home. Bert, her only living son, came from his home in Idaho for the funeral. Joseph Luff preached the sermon in Stone Church, and President Joseph Smith III assisted. Emma is buried in Independence beside her husband.

MARY

JANE

WARNKY

M^{ary} Jane Brownell, three years
old and very frightened, crawled
under the patchwork quilt and remained still. She could
hear the terrifying yells of the Indians who were circling
the covered wagon where she was hiding. After what
seemed a long time, things became quiet. She could hear
her mother calling to her. The Indian attack was over,
and the wagon train could continue on its way to
California.

The Brownells were moving from Council Bluffs,
Iowa, where Mary Jane had been born on September 3,
1848, to Sacramento, California. Here she spent her
childhood and grew to be an attractive young woman.

Here also she met Frederick C. Warnky, a German youth who had migrated to the United States.

When she moved with her parents to Oregon, Fred followed her. They were married in Corvallis on December 18, 1865, and returned to California to establish their home. They lived near a settlement of friendly Indians who enjoyed eating "white man's bread" while it was still oven-warm. Sometimes when the Indians smelled the fresh bread they would walk into the Warnky cabin and take a loaf. They did not consider this stealing but a gift of friendship from the Warnkys.

It was in California that Fred met W. W. Blair and Hervey Green, missionaries of the Reorganized Church. He and Mary Jane studied carefully the beliefs of this and other churches. They were baptized in 1868 by Elder E. C. Brand.

At a conference in the fall of 1874 it was decided to send Brother Warnky to Colorado as a missionary. Because Mary Jane enjoyed telling people that this church was the same as the one Jesus established on earth, and because she wanted to be with her husband, she moved with their small children to Colorado.

Missionary Warnky made a living for the family with his "traveling photography" business. Many of the photographs of Colorado in old history books were taken by him. While Mary Jane lived with friends or in a rented cabin, he would travel by team and wagon from mining camp to mining camp in the mountains, taking photographs and preaching the gospel. His spring wagon was covered to make both sleeping quarters and a workroom for developing and printing pictures. Sometimes Mary Jane and the children would travel with him. On these occasions they would set up a large tent as living quarters.

Fred Warnky was a friendly person the people enjoyed knowing. In two letters written in 1875 he said, "I find friends in this country in almost every place," and "I have calls from every direction to come and preach."

The Warnkys lived first in Greeley, Colorado, then in other localities. Mary Jane had many memorable experiences in this frontier state. One night when her husband was away she heard a loud commotion outside their cabin door. The dog barked furiously. When she started to open the door to find out the cause of the commotion, some unseen force seemed to pull her away. In the morning she found the dead bodies of a huge bear and her dog. If she had opened the door the animals might have continued their fierce fight inside the cabin.

Later the Warnkys got a rather nice house in Denver. The front room was quite large, so they made temporary seats and held preaching services every Sunday and some evenings of the week. Often Mary Jane went with Fred to visit their neighbors and to tell them about the church.

When they started a Sunday school in their house, Mary Jane did much of the work because Fred was away so often. With her four children assisting, she made a game of preparing the room for church services. On January 1, 1875, the Denver Branch was organized in this big room by Brother Warnky. Colorado had not yet become a state, and Mary Jane wanted her children to grow up in the United States, especially in the Center Place. The Colorado Saints promised, "We will support you and the children if you will remain here with us," but in November 1879 Mary Jane and the children moved by train to Independence. They were met at the station by the president of the Independence Branch, John W. Brackenbury, and were taken by wagon to his home. There they lived for three months until spring arrived.

During those three months Brother Warnky took his photography business to New Mexico and earned a considerable amount of money. Then he went to Independence, bought a house, moved his family in, and returned to New Mexico for another three months.

When he returned to Independence he started a photography business a short distance from the city square. To his studio came many people of the neighborhood and the church. Homesteaders moving west would often have their pictures taken here and sent back to their families.

The Warnkys attended the "Brick Church" where Mary Jane was a member of the Sisters' Aid Society. Later she became vice-president and in 1896 she was elected president. Four more children were born to the Warnky family in Independence.

Mary Jane had always enjoyed music and could play the organ. In 1881 the Warnkys got a new organ and the first choir of the Brick Church was organized in their home in October 1882. Their daughter Melissa was made the organist, with Mary Jane as her assistant.

The Saints attending the Brick Church were divided on whether or not the church should have an organ.

Some believed such music was evil and should not be permitted in the church building. The Warnkys were in favor of it. Shortly after the choir was organized, Brother Warnky and several other men went to Kansas City, Missouri, purchased an organ with their own money, and installed it in the church. Although some people still objected, Mary Jane delighted in having members of her family play the church organ and sing in the choir. For several years Brother Warnky served as the pastor of the church.

In the spring of 1887 Melissa was married in the Brick Church to Rudolph Etzenhouser, a member of a prominent church family. This was one of the last weddings to take place in the church.

The congregation was increasing so rapidly that a larger church was needed. At a branch business meeting on January 3, 1887, a building committee was selected. Brother Warnky served on it, and the first committee meeting was held in the Warnky photo studio.

On December 18, 1915, Mary Jane and Fred celebrated their golden wedding anniversary. Fred died December 24, 1920, just a few days after their fifty-fifth wedding anniversary.

A son-in-law of Sister Warnky said of her, "She never got cross as people do sometimes when they get old. The only complaint she made was that her age kept her from doing more work for the church and other people." Mary Jane Warnky, missionary wife and mother of thirteen children, was seventy-six when she died January 11, 1925. She is buried in Independence, Missouri.

EMMA

HOUGAS

A gray-haired, ninety-year-old woman sat in her comfortable chair in Resthaven, the church's home in Independence, Missouri, for elderly people, and wrote in her autobiography: "I have done nothing outstanding in my life."

Some years earlier she had written, "Our correspondence has been heavy, which is encouraging, since it manifests an awakening and shows the people are interested and ready to work." But that was the way with Emma Gamet Hougas—she was always anxious to be serving others and never expecting any recognition for herself.

She was born June 11, 1864, in Logan, Utah. Her parents, Solomon and Louisa Gamet, were members of the Church of Jesus Christ of Latter-day Saints. When she was five years old her parents left Utah and the church there. They moved to a farm near Little Sioux, Iowa, where her father's parents, David and Hanna Gamet, lived. These people had been members of the church in Nauvoo years before.

Grandfather Gamet owned a store and inn and operated the post office in Little Sioux. He was a bishop in the Reorganized Church. Emma grew to love her grandfather dearly. When a grown woman, she wrote about him, "Grandfather was my hero." Her father was a kind and good man, but when he left the church in Utah he had declared that he would never again join any church. Her mother united with the Reorganized Church while Emma was still too young for baptism.

The year she was eleven years old, her two older sisters married and moved into homes of their own. Only Emma was left to help her mother. She was so busy with school and work at home that she had little time for leisure.

She was baptized October 8, 1876, at Council Bluffs, Iowa. That same year she attended her first reunion. About this time her father also became a member of the church.

Emma wanted to become a schoolteacher, but her father said, "Stay home and help your mother. One of these days you will marry some nice young man. Stay here with us until then." But her mother said, "If Emma wants to teach school, she should be given a chance to do it. Because she is a woman she need not be confined to the house."

Arrangements were made for her to attend an advance school in Little Sioux, and for the next two years she lived with her grandparents. When she was eighteen, she taught her first school. Later she took additional training and taught at a college in Shenandoah, Iowa. Here she became acquainted with Thomas Augustus Hougas, also a member of the church. They were in the same graduation class.

Grandfather Gamet died in 1884 and her father took over management of the store in Little Sioux. Emma continued to teach school until 1889. Then on Christmas Day of that year, she married Thomas A. Hougas. They moved to a farm near Henderson, Iowa, and attended Farm Creek Branch, one of the oldest branches of the Reorganization. Emma taught in the Sunday school. At the time she and Tom started attending, a new church was being built. They helped with it.

Two sons were born to the Hougases—Almon (A. G.) in 1890 and Ward in 1895. Years later, Emma wrote of her sons in her autobiography: "Their church work is a source of satisfaction, and I look on it with gratitude in my soul."

In 1891 the General Sunday School Association was organized, and in 1896 her husband was made superintendent of the association. This event influenced the rest of their lives and the lives of their children.

Emma was a delegate from the Fremont District to the General Conference in 1895. It was rather unusual for women to serve as delegates at that time. In fact, because of difficult traveling conditions, few women even attended conference. It was also in 1893 that she became superintendent of the local church school and the superintendent of the Sunday School Association in the Fremont District.

In 1897 she also served as clerk for the Fremont District. The Hougas family regularly attended reunions, and the boys greatly enjoyed this. Years later Ward Hougas wrote: "We would always leave home in our covered wagon in the evening. A bed was made in the wagon so A. G. and I could sleep. About midnight we would stop to feed the horses and let them rest. Then we would continue traveling all night."

At reunions there were no classes for children or youth. Such classes were started but no child or teen-ager could attend unless he had the permission of a parent or guardian. At reunion Emma always sought the parents of her sons' playmates and asked if the children and youth could attend the classes arranged for their ages.

The Sunday School Association in which she served prepared and published the first Sunday school lessons. From this organization came the present Department of Religious Education. There were people who opposed having classes and services geared especially for children and youth. When parents would say, "Our children must stay with us in the preaching service," Brother and Sister Hougas would answer, "Then put adult clothes on them when they listen to an adult sermon. The fit is the same. Eventually, of course, the children will grow into them."

In 1903 Emma became the recording secretary of the Daughters of Zion for the General Church, and the following year she became superintendent of the Home Department of the Sunday School Association. She encouraged parents to send in questions to be answered, and urged people to have home classes. In her writing, she sometimes made the remark, "It is easy to aim at nothing . . . and hit it."

In 1906 the *Sunday School Exponent* was first published. T. A. Hougas served as the editor of the magazine while still continuing as the superintendent of the Sunday School Association. In addition to her work as the superintendent of the Home Department of the Sunday School Association, Emma became the editor of two columns in the *Sunday School Exponent,* one for the Home Department and one for parents. In 1908 she reported to the Sunday School Association, "At home we have attended to our correspondence and edited the *Sunday School Exponent.* We have done the best we could and all that we could. But notwithstanding we have employed every possible hour in the work, there remains much undone that should be done. We have not been able to keep our correspondence up. Letters come asking for instruction and we have not been able to respond as we should like." Later she wrote, "We have been permitted strength to do the work with the best of our knowledge. We have very much enjoyed the work, and the testimony of the Spirit that we are in the service of the Master is ample compensation."

A. G., her older son, recalling those days, wrote:

Editorial weeks were hectic. During the day we worked on the farm. In the evenings we worked on the *Exponent.* Hundreds of form letters were sent to home department leaders. A stencil was cut and the letters were run off on an old flat-bed mimeograph. After the stencil was well inked and working, a sheet of paper would be carefully put on the soapstone bed, the stencil rack turned down and the roller run over it. Each letter was then lifted off and laid out to dry. We boys helped with this. We would have copies of the letter drying on the stairs, on the furniture, and in rows on the floor. When they were dry we would fold them and put them in envelopes for mailing.

Emma Hougas was one of the women appointed in 1906 by church leadership to establish a children's home in Lamoni. The home was opened August 15, 1911. In 1912 she served as the social service chairman for the woman's auxiliary in the Fremont District. Her work was to organize women's groups in the district.

In 1920 the Farm Creek Branch was disorganized because members were moving away. The remaining Saints drove to Carson, Iowa, to attend church. Here T. A. was pastor, and Emma served in the Sunday school and with the women.

On April 15, 1932, Emma had a joy that few mothers experience. She saw her son, Ward, ordained president of the High Priests Quorum of the world church.

When T. A.'s health began to fail in 1944 they moved from St. Joseph to Warrensburg, Missouri, into an apartment in the Ward Hougas home. He died on July 24, 1946.

A few days after Christmas in 1949 Emma moved to Resthaven in Independence. This remained her home until her death on September 3, 1962. She was ninety-eight years old. She was buried beside her husband in Henderson, Iowa.

ANNA

OKERLIND

H er father was talking "religion" again and Anna laid her sewing down to listen. Her parents were very religious, but her father was not satisfied with the doctrine taught by the church they were attending. The Lundquist home was in Husby Herrgord, Husby Oppunda, Socermanland, Sweden. Anna was born there September 8, 1875.

By the time she was a young woman she had seven younger brothers and sisters. She went to work as a cook and maid for a wealthy family. Her parents had left their church and had become members of the Church of Jesus Christ of Latter-day Saints.

Anna was a good singer and dancer. "I would rather dance than eat," she often said. Mormon missionaries who were preaching near her home convinced her parents that she should migrate to Utah. They also told her that she would have to give up dancing because the church did not approve of it.

In June of 1900 she and several other young women made the long trip from Sweden to Salt Lake City. Anna felt comforted to be among so many people who shared her beliefs. However, at the first prayer meeting she attended in the local ward house, something unexpected happened. As soon as the prayer meeting ended the church members rolled back the rug, and a dance was held.

In Salt Lake City there was a church for people from Sweden. All of her friends were Swedish, and so she attended this church. Consequently, she did not learn to speak the English language, and she did not learn American culture.

Among her new friends were the three Okerlind sisters. She had become acquainted with their brother Oscar when he was a missionary in Sweden. In Utah the acquaintance was renewed and grew into love. Anna and Oscar were married February 19, 1902. Because they were dedicated church members they were married in a special ceremony in the temple. They entered the temple at 8:00 a.m. with great expectations and came out at 4:30 p.m. feeling depressed and bewildered. The marriage ceremony was not as they had thought it would be.

As part of the ceremony they were given secret names by which they were to be known in the next world. They discovered that every woman being married that day was given the name of Sarah, and every man the name of Peter. They did not agree with the belief

64

explained to them that the husband would go first into the life after death, and that if he wanted his wife with him he would call her secret name, and if he did not call her by the secret name, she would never be able to get into heaven.

One thing that particularly annoyed Anna was the loss of her new white shoes. At the beginning of the ceremony, she had to take them off and leave them on a shelf; during the service she wore temple slippers. When she and her new husband were ready to leave the temple she found that someone had taken her new shoes. As she walked away in her stocking feet, she was far from being a happy bride.

Disappointments continued, and eventually the Oker-linds stopped attending church. They found more and more things in the Utah church doctrine that annoyed them. Then some friends of theirs who had also come from Sweden said to them, "We have joined the Josephites." When Anna and Oscar asked who the "Josephites" were, the friends told them about the Reorganized Church.

A missionary for the Reorganized Church, Swen Swensen, began holding services in the little town of Sandy about four miles from the Okerlind home. Anna and Oscar and their friends went to hear him. They liked what they heard and did further investigating. Elder Swensen, who had come from Sweden, preached in their native tongue.

The Okerlinds were baptized in 1904 while still living in Salt Lake City. In 1906 Oscar was asked to serve in Utah as a missionary. The following year he was sent on a mission to Sweden. It was decided by the church that

Anna and their three daughters should move to Independence, Missouri.

When Oscar was ready to leave he found that he had barely enough money to reach Sweden, but the bishop said the church could not afford to give him more. Anna gave him the last of her savings so that he could buy new shoes for the journey. When he reminded her that she also needed shoes, she answered, "I will be going no place but church."

Three other families who had lived in Utah also united with the Reorganized Church and moved to Independence. None of them spoke English, and because of this they were shunned by some of the members. When the three girls started playing with the children of the neighborhood and attending school, they learned the English language. From her daughters Anna began to learn it too. Every Sunday afternoon the family attended the prayer meetings at Stone Church.

Two Swedish brothers, Fred and John Lund, and their families moved from California to Independence. Immediately these families became friendly with the Okerlinds. Anna and her daughters always spent Christmas and special days with the Lunds. Others became more friendly too. Following Christmas in 1909 Anna put this message in a local newspaper: "Notice of appreciation. To whom it may concern—I hereby take the privilege to extend my thanks to the party who sent groceries received at my home on Christmas Eve. Your sister in Christ. Anna Okerlind."

In the meantime Oscar was busy with his missionary assignment in Sweden. He organized four Sunday schools, and wrote in a letter that he would like these schools to "become part of the general body" of the Sunday School Association.

When he returned from his mission in Sweden he was ordained a seventy in a service at Stone Church January 23, 1910. That same year he was assigned to Northeastern and Northwestern Kansas District. In a letter he wrote, "I was glad to get my field of labor this year so close to my home." That winter sorrow came to Anna. Her four-day-old son died. Anna's three daughters became even more dear to her after this loss.

In 1912 Oscar again returned to Sweden. Anna longed to see her loved ones in her old home, but she and her daughters remained in Independence. The church home for the aged was not far away and she often visited these people. Among other services she would do their laundry and have her daughter run errands for them. When church members moved from Sweden to Independence, Anna always invited them to her home, did their washings, and helped them become acquainted with the customs of the United States.

The girls attended school and church. Anna made clothes for them and cooked good meals. Sometimes, after a letter had come from Sweden, the girls would ask about that far-away country, and she would tell them about her childhood.

After three years in Sweden, Oscar came home again. It was a happy time for Anna when her husband rejoined the family. After that he was away frequently but only on brief missions. He was superannuated in 1946 and the family had a few years together before his death on July 16, 1949.

One of the Okerlind daughters writes, "In all the

years Father was in the mission field, we never heard Mother complain. After he died, she said, 'Now when we could be together, he has been taken away.' That was the nearest to any complaint we ever heard from her."

Anna and the girls continued to live in Independence until her death following a stroke on April 29, 1955. Both Anna and Oscar are buried in Independence.

MIRIAM

BRAND

ATWOOD

M iriam Abraham laid her sewing
on her lap, stretched her weary
back, and looked out over the ocean. She hoped she was
doing the right thing in leaving her native England. She
and four hundred other church members had left
Liverpool on December 12, 1854, bound for the United
States.

Born April 1, 1832, at Devizes, England, she was the
only member of her family making the voyage. She was
not strong, and it was hoped that the mountain air of
Utah would help her.

Turning her gaze from the ocean to an attractive
young man standing in front of her, she recognized

Edmund C. Brand, a diligent church worker and the ship's doctor. "Sister, there is a button off my coat. Would you sew it on for me?"

"Gladly," agreed Miriam. She looked at the thread still clinging to the button. It had been cut. The young man smiled and said, "I'm guilty. I cut the thread so I could make an excuse to start a conversation with you."

As she sewed, they talked. He too had been born and baptized in England. They discussed Zionic conditions and wondered about what they would find in Salt Lake City. The voyage took a month and by the time the ship docked in New Orleans, Louisiana, they had become close friends.

With other Saints they boarded a riverboat and went up the Mississippi River to St. Louis, Missouri. Miriam remained in St. Louis with church members while Edmund went farther north. When he found employment he sent for her immediately. They were married May 2, 1855, and only a few days later started with a wagon train for Salt Lake City. He drove a team of oxen and did other work on the journey. Miriam cooked for a number of men. This meant lifting heavy iron kettles and cooking out of doors with limited supplies.

By the time they reached Salt Lake City, it was November and the weather was cold. Like all newcomers to the valley, they had to be baptized again. They had crossed the ocean believing that the church was the same as the original, but they found that new doctrines had been added.

After several months in Salt Lake City they decided they could not accept these new doctrines. In the fall they moved to a community outside the city and started to build a house but both of them became ill.

In the winter of 1856-57 certain leaders of the Utah church instigated "the reform." Miriam and her husband attended the meetings of this religious revival in hopes they could renew their faith. They were even baptized again, but they still were not happy with their religion. Troops of United States soldiers quartered in Utah during the federal conflict with the Mormons offered to protect those who wanted to leave Utah territory. With this protection, the young couple moved to California.

Here they determined to have nothing more to do with the church. Miriam opened a store where she sold fancywork that she and other women made. Business was so good she had to hire help. Her husband had a promising business as a dentist and doctor. They were prosperous and happy. But in June of 1863 they were given a spiritual experience. The following December they learned about the Reorganization. At first they argued with the young man who brought the message to them, but a few days later they were baptized—the first man and woman to join the church in San Francisco. They immediately opened their home for missionary services, and Miriam studied the doctrine of the church so she could explain it to those who visited her shop.

Then the call came for her husband to become a missionary. Although Miriam hated to sacrifice her business and their pleasant life together, she closed her shop, sold the furniture, and stayed in the homes of friends while he traveled on foot as a missionary in California. Sometimes she went with him. On one occasion, while they were walking twelve miles to make a missionary visit, they sat down on a log to rest. "I'm hungry and thirsty," said Miriam. "Why doesn't the

Lord feed us as he did the Israelites in the wilderness?" Immediately a wagon came racing toward them. The driver stopped the horses near them and began tossing big red apples until her lap overflowed. "That is enough," she called. The man drove away and the grateful travelers quenched their thirst and satisfied their hunger. Miriam believed they had been given divine assistance.

In 1866 Alexander H. Smith, brother of Joseph Smith III, visited California. Because they had discovered conflicting information about the missionary who had first told them of the Reorganization, and because they wanted to be baptized by one of the priesthood with authority, the Brands were baptized again—Edmund in November of 1866 and Miriam the following month.

The next spring Edmund was asked to go on a mission to Nevada. Miriam did not want to leave California but she wanted to be with Edmund so she said farewell to friends, realizing she might never see them again. The Brands made their home and headquarters in Austin, Nevada.

Because a farmer received healing under the hands of Brother Brand, he presented a beautiful horse to him. For years Brother Brand rode this horse on his missions.

When the church asked him to go to Utah, Miriam predicted, "That mission will cost you your life. You will be called an apostate for leaving that church." But a few months later they moved to Utah. Saints in Nevada loaned them another horse and a wagon on condition they sell them in Utah and send the money back to the Nevada Saints. On the way they had to cross a desert.

The sun beat hot and the sand was deep. The horses strained under the extreme heat. Miriam's tongue swelled and her lips cracked. One of the horses staggered and fell exhausted. While her husband tended the animal, Miriam went to one side to pray. Only a miracle could keep them from perishing. A voice said to her, "Look behind the sand hill." She did and found a large barrel of clear, cool water, almost buried in the sand. She removed the lid and drank from her cupped hand. Then she ran to Edmund, calling about the water. He paid little attention to her words, for he reasoned she was out of her head from being in the extreme heat. When she grabbed a bucket from their wagon, he followed her. Before tasting the water, he knelt in gratitude. She had forgotten to do that. They carried water to their horses and filled every container in their wagon. For the rest of the way they had drinking water, but when they reached green fields and farmland again, the water became bitter.

They had no trouble selling the horse and wagon, but they did have trouble finding a place to live. Miriam went often with her husband on preaching assignments.

She also visited in the homes of women she formerly knew and told them about the Reorganization.

Certain members of the Mormon church did many things to frighten and annoy Miriam when she was alone in the house. When her husband bought a large Newfoundland dog to protect her, the dog was poisoned. At last it was decided that she should move east to live while he finished his assignment to Utah. She and another woman traveled by train to Council Bluffs, Iowa. In the fall of 1871 her husband joined her and they bought a farm near Tabor. Edmund continued to travel on the horse he had been given in the West as he did missionary work in the midwestern states. He and Elder J. S. Lee held missionary services in May of 1873 in the courthouse in Independence, Missouri.

An unexpected joy came to Miriam in 1885. Her sister's son, Charles Fry, a boy thirteen years old, came from England to live with the Brands. She now had company while her husband was away and someone to help her on the farm. The following spring Charles was baptized by his uncle.

In October 1890 E. C. Brand died while on a mission to Kansas. Charles continued to live with his aunt, and she did all she could to encourage him to serve the church.

About 1894 she moved to Independence, Missouri. Her nephew was now a man, and a dedicated member of the priesthood. Several hymns which he wrote are in *The Hymnal.*

Despite poor health, she remarried and for the remainder of her life found happiness as the wife of Elder Atwood. She died August 24, 1899. Funeral services were held in the Stone Church, and burial was in Independence.

CHARLOTTE

CHEVILLE

Just after the death of Charlotte Cheville, a good friend said, "What do you suppose Grandma Cheville is doing now?" The quick answer of another friend was, "Singing." And that is the way it always was. Some people sing as a result of training; Charlotte sang for joy.

Charlotte was born in a small village in Yorkshire, England, February 26, 1872. Her parents, George and Mary Backous, had five sons and four daughters. George was a laborer in a factory, and income was limited. As soon as the children were old enough they were "let out" to work. Charlotte began assisting in homes when she was ten.

Her father was rotund and stern. Her mother was small and jolly and liked to sing to her children. Neither parent belonged to a church, but every Sunday the children attended classes at a nearby Methodist church.

At this time many people in England were immigrating to the United States. Three of Charlotte's brothers went to Iowa to live. Charlotte liked to read the long, interesting letters they sent home. The brothers persuaded their parents to move to the United States. Only an older son and daughter remained in England.

It took two weeks to cross the ocean, and the constant movement of the ship made Charlotte sick. Then there was the long train ride from New York City to Marshall, Iowa.

The brothers and other relatives made the family welcome in their new land. Many of the people living near their home were English.

Charlotte went to work in the household of a family that had recently moved from England. The farm was large and there was much work for her to do, but the people were kind and considerate. When they went to visit relatives they took her with them. There she met George Cheville, a young man who worked on the farm of the relatives. He had been born in Canada, but his parents had come from England. His parents had died when he was young, leaving him younger brothers and sisters to support. He was short, energetic, and friendly. Her respect for him developed into love and they were married February 25, 1887.

Their first home was a log cabin near Maxwell, Iowa. Because they had no well of their own, they had to carry water a long distance. Later they were able to purchase a farm which they called Pleasant Hill. They also bought livestock and built a new house and barn. And they had their own well. Charlotte enjoyed nature and carefully tended her vegetable garden and flower beds. But the Chevilles' most cherished possessions were their three daughters and two sons. The rural school the children attended was a mile from Pleasant Hill. Every Sunday the children walked a mile in the opposite direction to attend a Protestant church school.

Charlotte was a good wife and mother. Like her own mother she sang as she worked and delighted in having her children sing also. The atmosphere of the Cheville household was pleasant. Parents and children worked, studied, laughed, and loved as they lived together.

When George Cheville's health began to fail, they sold the farm and moved to the small town of Rhodes, Iowa.

Several families who belonged to the Reorganized Church lived in the Rhodes area. They became friends of the Chevilles. In January 1914 two missionaries, J. L. Parker and D. J. Williams, held a series of services in a hall in Rhodes. Friends invited the Chevilles to attend these meetings. They were pleased with the services and became interested in the church. Two of the children asked to be baptized—Roy, sixteen, a high school student, and Cora, eighteen. Brother Parker visited the Cheville home to speak to the parents about the requested baptisms. Both Charlotte and her husband declared, "If they want to join the church, it is their right to make the decision."

Charlotte watched as Roy and Cora were baptized in a small lake that was used as a railroad reservoir. It was a cold day in January and the ice had to be cut before the baptismal service could take place. As she watched the service, she thought deeply of the doctrine of this church and became more convinced that it was the restored church of Christ. On January 21, 1915 she was baptized and confirmed by Brother Parker at Rhodes, Iowa. Her husband, always a good companion and father, attended church but never became a member. Later two other children, Fred and Mildred, also joined.

Members living in and near Rhodes purchased a lot in 1914 on which to build a church but in the summer of 1915 they bought a country schoolhouse to move to the site. The Cheville family joined the picnic held on July 4, 1915, and helped to tear down the schoolhouse and haul the parts to the vacant lot. Two years later, on December 39, 1917, the church was dedicated.

Sister Cheville was asked to sing in the choir, and she enjoyed this. At first she was too self-conscious to look up. But she continued to sing and eventually mastered the music. When she was asked to sing in a quartet, she prayed and practiced. Her children and husband encouraged her. "You can do it," they said. "Pretend you are ironing clothes and singing to yourself." Then she went on to sing solos. Often at a wedding, a funeral, or other special occasion, the request would be, "Ask Aunt Charlotte to sing."

She recognized the importance of a patriarchal blessing and received hers on October 18, 1921. The words given in the blessing are ample proof of the righteousness of this good woman.

In the sweetness of your temperament, . . . you may witness to others that your God has been working with you all the days of your life. . . . God shall bless your offspring after you, till they shall in many instances bring honor and glory to the name of God and in this your name as parent shall yet be honored. . . . You have known trials and at times your burdens of life have been heavy; but God has strengthened you so you would not give way under the troubles of life. Fear not; out of all shall come good to you and to your family.

When she was eighty-five years old she suffered a severe paralytic stroke and was not expected to live. She went to a small home for older persons and there recovered. She massaged her hand and practiced speaking; she would not surrender to invalidism. Her speech returned; her left hand and arm became usable again. Nurses would bring her mending for their children's clothes, and she would do it gladly.

Her mind was clear and her interest in reading never lessened. She took the *Herald* and read it consistently. She would say, "I want to keep up on what's going on."

The Christmas following her stroke her son Roy, who had become the Presiding Patriarch of the church, said, "Mother, we are going to sing a duet."

"Oh, Roy," she protested, "my voice is no longer suitable for singing . . . but we can try." Together they sang for the other people of the home, "The Old, Old Path," "Star in the East," and "Away in a Manger."

On November 13, 1966, at the age of ninety-five, Sister Cheville died. A great-grandson—a little fellow—was perplexed about what had happened to his grandmother. Then when he went to the cemetery and saw the tent erected over the grave, he said delightedly, "I know where Grandma is. . . . She has gone camping." To him camping was something wonderful, and he could visualize his great-grandmother enjoying the singing and the out of doors.

Charlotte Cheville was the type of woman, wife, mother, and grandmother needed in the church of Jesus Christ.

LYDIA

WIGHT

Five-year-old Lydia Thomas rolled over in bed and listened to the pleasant sound of her father and mother singing in harmony. Fascinated, she got out of her bed and went to the top of the stairs so she could hear better.

Her father was a missionary for the Reorganized Church. Lydia, her older brother, and her younger sister always enjoyed those times when their father came home and brought the portable organ. He had been a teacher before becoming a missionary.

Sitting at the top of the stairs that night, Lydia looked down with admiration at her parents. Her father

81

invited her to join in the singing. Then she began to cultivate her stewardship of music. Soon thereafter her father gave the children lessons in rudimentary music whenever he was home. Later they secured an old organ, and Lydia found it a pleasure to practice.

Born at Pleasanton, Iowa, on March 19, 1888, Lydia and her family traveled to Leon, Iowa, to attend church. After the Sunday morning chores were done on their small acreage they drove to services by horse and buggy. Often they were the first to arrive.

Several years after Lydia was baptized, the family moved to Lamoni where they could live among church people. Here her mother had less heavy work to do, but the family still kept an orchard and a garden. When Lydia was in high school, her mother became ill. Relatives suggested that Lydia quit school to take care of her mother, but her mother said emphatically, "I did not receive a good education. Lydia is going to have one, and she is going to make use of it." By doing extra assignments, Lydia completed four years of schooling in three years.

After high school graduation in 1906, she attended Graceland College and two summer sessions at Iowa Teachers College. Then she taught grade school in Lamoni for three years. The next two years she attended Iowa University, majoring in English. She had a scholarship for tuition, and some friends loaned her money. She worked for her room and board and did sewing and other work to pay expenses. She was a member of the University Women's Glee Club and sang in the Vesper Choir and the Oratorio Chorus. She was also a choir member at the Methodist Church for both years. When she returned to Lamoni she taught in the high school. At church she taught a class of young men.

On June 14, 1914, she became the bride of Leslie S. Wight, son of Apostle and Mrs. J. W. Wight. They made their home in Lamoni and she continued to teach in the high school there for a year. In 1915 she was asked to teach a correspondence course in English composition offered by Graceland College. Several members of the traveling ministry enrolled. She was still serving in this capacity when her first son was born.

When Les went into the army in 1918, she returned to teaching in the high school. A friend kept house for them, and Lydia's mother had a small apartment in the home. (Her father had died previously.) After Les returned from service he went into sales work. In 1919 a second son was born. When he was three years old the family moved to Kansas City, Missouri, but a year later returned to Lamoni.

The Wights were interested in Graceland College and took students into their home to live. One was Pataha Samuela, the Tahitian youth who came to the United States when Apostle and Sister Clyde Ellis returned home after their mission in the islands.

President F. M. Smith asked Lydia Wight to serve on the education commission of the world church. This meant she was to make suggestions for enlarging Graceland's field of service. Two of her suggestions were accepted. One was to add a geology department; the other was that the music department should offer training for public school music teachers.

While they lived in Lamoni, both Lydia and Les were busy in church work. Years later she wrote: "We went to alternate meetings so we could change off caring for the boys while they were too young to take. We'd laugh as we passed each other coming or going to the Brick Church one block away. As Les returned Sunday afternoon from a priesthood meeting, I left for choir practice. We got along fine and the boys seemed to enjoy the arrangement."

One of Lydia's outstanding projects was the Mother-craft Class. One group of mothers met on Sunday during the church school hour. Another group, who could not attend on Sunday morning, left their babies with their husbands one evening a week to take the course. The classes grew. When some of the husbands asked to share in the Sunday morning study, Alonzo Jones of the Graceland faculty was secured as instructor. Girls from the college cared for the small children, and babies were taken to a nursery supervised by Dona Haden in the Wight home a block from the church. Over fifty people regularly attended these Sunday classes.

When her husband's business necessitated their moving to Minneapolis, Minnesota, Lydia was very disheartened over having to leave her church work. The gloom lifted when she arrived and found that the pastor had already made arrangements for her to serve as church school director in the branch in Minneapolis. She had done this type of work before in other places where they had lived.

Dr. F. M. McDowell of the Department of Religious Education asked her in 1939 to test new education policies in her church school. Under her direction, much of the material used thereafter in religious education was evaluated.

She and another woman conducted a weekday nursery school in the Wight home. From this enterprise there developed another class for parents. Skilled medical men, fathers of some of the pupils, helped to instruct the class.

While living in Minneapolis she was asked to help the Department of Religious Education by serving as editor of church school quarterlies. Les adjusted his work so they could move to Independence, Missouri. For three years she edited materials for children, young people, and adults. Many of the quarterlies she helped prepare are still treasured by church members. She revised old writings and created new. Besides working on quarterlies, she helped to edit *Guidelines to Leadership* and various booklets.

She was sent as a representative of Herald House to a number of religious education institutes held in different cities by other publishers of religious materials. She often conducted teacher-training classes at church institutes, reunions, and conferences.

While she was working at Herald House, her mother—still living in Lamoni—became extremely ill. One day when Lydia mentioned that she might resign to help, her mother declared, "No, Lydia. It was for this purpose that I insisted you get an education. Continue your work for the church. I'll be all right." Lydia took the manuscript on which she was working back to the publishing house, and that same day her mother died.

The next home of the Wights was in Chicago, Illinois. Here Lydia served as the district women's leader. In this capacity she had to travel to other cities in the district to teach classes and help with institutes. She also became church school director for First Chicago Branch. Her husband was patriarch in two districts at this time, and they often visited in the homes of the Saints. She trained people to assist her with the work of directing the church school of the branch. She also helped to organize the vacation school of the First Chicago Branch in 1956.

She died May 2, 1962, in Chicago.

JENNIE

Z.

ELLIOTT

The frail little woman who was being baptized could not see Elder J. C. Stuart or the baptismal font in the Central Church of Kansas City. The woman was blind.

Jennie Zelma Elliott was born at Laclede, Missouri, on April 30, 1890. An unfortunate event in early childhood caused her gradually to lose her sight. She was not able to attend school as other children, but her parents did all they could to help her.

When she was junior age, her favorite pastime was to create stories and tell them to other children. Because she could not write, she committed these stories to memory.

When she was about eight years old, she heard of "seeing-eye dogs" and decided to train the family pet, a large dog, to become her "seeing eye." She did not tell her parents what she was doing. She tied a rope around the friendly dog and took him outside. "Now," she explained to the dog, "you walk easy and lead me around the big trees in this yard. We will walk all over this yard together." The dog was kind but he did not understand the situation. Seeing a rabbit he ran off, dragging Jennie behind him. She screamed and tried to stop him, but he kept on running. When he turned a corner suddenly Jennie landed in the middle of some bushes. She was frightened, bruised, and lost. A neighbor woman came to her rescue and took her home. Jennie and the dog remained friends, but she never again tried to make him her seeing eye.

Her parents moved to Illinois when she was a young woman, and there she attended a school for the blind. She learned to read and write Braille. After she completed training at the school, she took Braille correspondence courses in creative writing. She enjoyed writing stories in which the main character was blind.

When she was a grown woman she went to live at the Catherine Hale Home in Kansas City, Missouri. Saints who were members of Central congregation in Kansas City often visited this home and assisted the residents to attend church services. It was through some of these visiting Saints that Jennie first heard about the restored gospel. They took her to services at the church and explained the doctrine to her. They visited her in her room at the home and read church literature to her.

Elder Herbert Lively and his wife, Mary, who visited

her often, said, "Reading to Sister Elliott was always an uplifting experience." The Livelys made a special effort to spend part of every Christmas Day with her, helping her open her gifts. (Elder Lively was at the time pastor of Central congregation in Kansas City, Missouri.)

Jennie Elliott was baptized March 27, 1948, in Kansas City. Soon after her baptism, she wrote a story and sent it to one of the church papers. It was published in *Stepping Stones*. The editors of Herald House invited her to contribute more material. Her writings were published in *Saints' Herald, Daily Bread, The Skylark Leader, Stepping Stones,* and *Zion's Hope.* Leonard Lea, editor of the *Herald* at that time, said of Jennie: "She can accomplish more without sight than many of us can with good eyes."

The Oriole and Skylark organizations of the Englewood congregation in Independence, Missouri, once went by caravan to visit Sister Elliott and present a program for the women in the Catherine Hale Home. There were ten cars full of girls and their parents. Sister Elliott was concerned because she thought the younger Skylark girls would avoid her because the pupils of her blind eyes were very large and out of proportion to the normal pupil of an eye. Instead the girls were eager to be near her and to hold her hand while she walked.

At the 1956 World Conference she demonstrated to a large number of people how to read and write in Braille. She and her Braille writer were brought from Kansas City to the Auditorium. People gathered around her asking many questions. This was truly a highlight in her life.

When the General Church began the program of

Ministry to the Blind, under the direction of Thelona Stevens, Jennie was asked to assist. On her Braille writer she prepared leaflets and tracts about church doctrine for the blind to read. In a letter to Leonard Lea she wrote, "How thrilled I was when Brother Al Scherer came one afternoon with one of the tracts the Denver folks had Brailled. It is the one entitled, 'You Should Read the Book of Mormon.' It is beautifully done. But he was not bringing the book just for me to see. He wants me to make an extra copy or two of it. I was a little hesitant because I am a better Braille reader than writer. If I do this job satisfactorily, I'll do as many more as they want me to."

Another letter of hers was published in the *Herald* for September 28, 1959:

When I went down to my noonday meal on April 1, 1958, I little thought that within a few minutes time my whole life would be changed. But so it was, for as I was sitting down to the table I fell and broke my left hip. I was rushed to Kansas City's General Hospital, where I was a patient for sixteen weeks. My doctor told me that, although it usually took more than six weeks for a broken bone to heal, he wanted me to remain in the hospital for twelve weeks before going to physical therapy for walking lessons. Then the evening before the twelve weeks were up he surprised me by saying he was sending me home because it was doubtful that I would ever walk again, so there was no need of my being there any longer. But the matron would not let me come back because she said she could not take care of me. Catherine Hale Home had been my only residence for more than twenty-one years. Where else could I go? What else could I do? These were questions I could not answer, even with the help of prayer.

And then early Sunday morning while I was wondering what would become of me, Jesus came and stood beside my bed. I could feel him reach down and take my left hand in his hand. I could not see him or hear his voice, yet I knew beyond all doubt he was there and that I need not worry any more. My prayer was answered, for I had his assurance that I would walk again and that I would be going home. Just a few days after this beautiful experience I changed doctors. Three days later I was in physical therapy, starting to walk. And on July 24 friends brought me home to my very own room, and to the home's new matron who was glad to have me. Although I have been home from the hospital more than a year, I am still very much a shut-in because I cannot go up and down stairs alone. But whenever I get discouraged and feel sorry for myself because I cannot get around as well as I think I ought, I remember that once a doctor told me that I would never walk again. He did not take into account what prayer and faith can do.

As a much older woman Jennie Z. Elliott moved to the nursing home in Independence, Missouri, operated by Brother and Sister David Binger, Sr. Here she died on January 5, 1960.

MABEL

SANFORD

ATKINSON

Years after the death of Mabel Sanford Atkinson her children and grandchildren sat on the bank of the Mississippi River at Nauvoo, Illinois, and made a tape recording of their memories of her. "We realize the value of the church in her life," said one. "Without the wide perspective Grandmother had about life she would never have been able to have completed the work she did," said another.

On June 13, 1882, Mabel Adelina Fairclough was born in Worchester, Massachusetts. Her parents had moved from England during their first year of married life and lived in a tenement area where there were many

Jewish families with whom they became close friends. Mabel often wished that instead of living in an apartment, they could have a country home so she could keep pets. The best she could do was to catch a little mouse and keep it in a bottle. Mabel had a younger sister named Daisy and a younger brother named Herbert.

Her mother, whose education had been limited because one had to pay to go to school in England in those days, knew the importance of an education and impressed this upon her children. They enjoyed music. Her mother, who had been taught to play the piano by her grandmother, gave Mabel lessons. The family spent many happy evenings around the piano singing favorite songs.

Mrs. Fairclough had a desire to find a church for her children. "I wish there was a church now," she would say, "like the church of Christ in the New Testament."

She found that church in a unique way. Mr. Fairclough, who had little interest in religion, visited Brother and Sister John Hoxie in regard to his insurance business, and during the conversation they quoted scriptures. "You sound like my wife," Mr. Fairclough said. "She quotes scripture and has the children doing it, too."

When Mrs. Hoxie asked what church Mrs. Fairclough belonged to, he told her that his wife was searching for a church to join that was like the New Testament church. "Then I must tell her about ours," declared the woman. "It is called the Reorganized Church of Jesus Christ of Latter Day Saints."

Not long after this Sister Hoxie visited the Fairclough home, taking books for the family to read.

After attending a number of church services and studying, Mrs. Fairclough, Mabel, Daisy, and Herbert were baptized on December 2, 1894. They became members of the branch at Boston, Massachusetts. Mabel was twelve years old then.

Services were held in a dance hall. Every Sunday mother and children walked to church and home afterwards. The father rarely attended; in fact, he sometimes made it unpleasant for his wife and children to attend. About nine years later, however, he was baptized also.

An avid reader, Mabel also enjoyed writing stories and poetry. One of the first stories she wrote was about the pet mouse in a bottle that she had had as a child.

Her sister Daisy, never very strong, died at the age of fourteen. Because the mother feared death might also take Mabel, she took her to a doctor. He said that her lungs were weak, and that she needed a lot of fresh air. Mabel, a seventh grader who loved school, had to terminate her education. But there were compensations; her mother bought bicycles, and every afternoon the two of them went riding together.

As a young woman, Mabel did something so unusual for a woman in the early 1900's that her picture was put in the local newspaper. She went to work as a public stenographer. In order to do this, she attended a business school where she received the necessary training. She gave private music lessons to earn money to pay for this special education.

Then romance came. At Fisher Business College

which she attended in Boston was a young instructor, Albert L. Sanford. He was a member of the church who had moved from Nova Scotia to Boston. (He was a nephew of Emma Burton.) Albert and Mabel were married in Boston, Massachusetts, on December 22, 1904.

During the years that followed three children were born to them—Florence, Mildred, and Albert, Jr. (generally called Jack). They enjoyed their home, their school, and their church activities. Many times they attended reunions. The tent and camping equipment were packed into a huge box and shipped by train to the location of the reunion; the family traveled by train also.

Although she was a busy mother and wife, Mabel wanted more education. Fisher Business College allowed her to study at home and take her final tests at the college. As she cooked meals and cleaned house, she found time to study. She also entered stories she had written in contests, and she won prizes.

When the Sanfords moved to a country place about ten miles from Boston, their way of living changed. The church was so far away they could no longer attend services, so Mabel conducted church school for the children in a home. The public school was also several miles away and Mabel arranged with the county school superintendent to teach the children at home. At the end of the year, when he gave the examinations, all three of the Sanford children proved to be capable students.

Later Mabel and Albert bought a car, and every Sunday they went to church in it. Then, during World

War I, the Sanford family moved to Independence where Mabel's parents were already living. She and the children went first, traveling by train. They lived in the home of her parents near the Sanitarium.

It was Conference time, and they were thrilled to see leaders of the church that they had read about in the *Saints' Herald*. Because the Auditorium was not yet built, Conference sessions were held in the Stone Church.

Several months later Brother Sanford also moved to Independence and the family moved to a place on West College Street. This was then on the edge of town with vacant lots and open field beyond. Brother Sanford found employment in the Liberty Bond Department at the Federal Reserve Bank in Kansas City, Missouri.

Boston friends of the Sanford children had said to them, "Missouri is so far away. Wild Indians must live there." But the greatest difficulty they encountered was the amusement their school mates showed at their Boston accent.

Excited at the opportunity of once more furthering her education, Mabel enrolled in the Institute of Art and Science sponsored by the church in Independence. Two of her teachers were Ida Etzenhouser and Ruby Short McKim. The latter taught art, and it was in one of these art classes that Mabel designed the cover used on a book *The Fourth Relaford* which was published by Herald House. At the same school Albert taught bookkeeping, accounting, shorthand, and typing in evening classes.

Both Albert and Mabel did extensive work in the church's program for children in Independence. He served as the director of all church schools in Independence and for several years was superintendent of the church school at Stone Church. Two of his assistants were Chris B. Hartshorn and Howard W. Harder. Mabel assisted with the church school, taught classes, led music, and played the piano.

President F. M. Smith was concerned about the number of children who attended church services but could get little value from sermons gauged for adults. He asked Albert Sanford to pioneer a new project for the church—special services for children. These were held in the Stone Church at the 11:00 o'clock hour immediately following the church school. Between one and two hundred children attended every Sunday. Special activities and sermons tailored for juniors made this a popular innovation.

It was at these junior services that Mabel Sanford learned to be a "story-teller" and developed her talent for writing programs and plays for children to present. Her daughter, when grown, said, "I remember seeing Mamma standing in front of our full-length mirror practicing the story she was to tell." Frequently she wrote her own stories.

Because children who had grown too old to attend the junior services were reluctant to leave, another special group was established. In 1922 the Sanfords took the twelve-and-under children while Walter W. Smith conducted services for teen-agers.

Interesting things were happening in Nauvoo, Illinois, too. Tourists were stopping there wanting to see the house where Emma and Joseph Smith, Jr., had lived. An aunt and uncle of Albert Sanford were asked by the church to move to Nauvoo and repair the Old Homestead, the Mansion House, and other buildings so tourists could visit them. These relatives, the John Laytons, wrote to the Sanfords about Nauvoo. "Chickens are being allowed to roost in the kitchen of the Old Homestead where Emma once prepared meals," they said, "and fishermen are spreading their wet nets to dry on the floor of the Nauvoo House."

One Conference when the Laytons were in Independence, they told such interesting things about Nauvoo that the Sanfords decided to visit Nauvoo. That was in 1921, and they traveled by train and stern-wheeler riverboat on the Mississippi. They found Nauvoo so rich in church history that they hated to return home.

Another summer they returned to Nauvoo, this time staying in the Nauvoo House. They could hear the water of the river moving against the shore every night. And as the girls scrubbed the big, rough floor of the kitchen they recalled how Emma had scrubbed this same floor. Because of this deep feeling for the place the Sanfords decided to move to Nauvoo. A farewell reception was held for them June 1, 1923, at the Stone Church. Brother Sanford was presented a gold watch chain, and Sister Sanford was given a copy of *Zion's Praises*.

The only employment Albert could find in Nauvoo was lettering gravestones. When the bodies of Joseph Smith, Jr., Hyrum Smith, and Emma Smith were buried side by side in the small cemetery on the Old Homestead, he cut the letters on the three stones. (These have been replaced by one long marker.)

When the Laytons first moved to Nauvoo in 1918 they were the only members of the church there. Later the Lees, the Fusselmans, and other Saints joined them.

These few members purchased an old brick schoolhouse and converted it into a church.

Mabel Sanford thrilled at the church history she discovered. She met James Gifford, the man who had rowed Joseph Smith III and Emma Smith across the Mississippi River when they went to Amboy, Illinois, in April 1860 to the General Conference. "It was such a bad day with such a strong wind," he told her, "that nobody wanted to make the trip. I said if Alexander would help me row the boat, we could make it. And we did. Emma and Joseph were drenched with spray by the time they got out of the boat."

Mabel visited people who had been neighbors of the Smiths. One man told her how as a boy he had fallen into the river and Emma had taken him into the house, dried his clothing, and let him wear Young Joseph's clothes in the meantime. Another said, "I remember Emma Smith's cookie jar. All of us boys were treated from it." One woman, Sophia Harsh, told how Emma had befriended her mother when she had come as a lone immigrant girl from Germany, and had later helped with her wedding.

Mabel taught her children to play the piano and violin. In fact, they formed a string ensemble that played at Parent-Teacher Association meetings. People seeing them would say, "If that is the kind of families in that church, then it must be a good church."

The Sanfords entered wholeheartedly into community activities. The older daughter, Florence, was elected president of the Young People's Christian Association, an organization composed of the youth of

Protestant churches in Nauvoo. Albert was elected president of the local PTA.

From 1924 to 1928 Mabel was *Saints' Herald* correspondent and sent in a monthly newsletter from Nauvoo. Then she began to write more extensively. She revised some of the programs and stories she had used in Independence, sent them to publishers, and sold them. She wrote programs and pageants that were presented in the Nauvoo church.

She took a correspondence course in story writing. Years later a daughter recalled, "Often at mealtime Mother would read to Father so he could give her advice. Not only was this interesting to us children but listening to willing and helpful suggestions was an education in itself."

Her typewriter was precious to her and she did not permit the children to play with it. Whenever the family went away for a few days she would hide it in the oven of the old kitchen range so it would not be found if a thief broke into the house.

One summer Ralph Farrell, who was also from the Boston Branch, served as a guide at the Joseph Smith homes. He said to her, "Mabel, you should write a book about the history of Nauvoo." She replied that it was a suitable subject for a book but that she was too busy with her home and church work. She taught children's classes in the church for many years and was in charge of the children's division in Nauvoo.

Then sorrow came. On April 29, 1935, at the age of fifty-five Albert Sanford died. He was buried in Nauvoo.

Mabel was grief-stricken for many months and wished she could die also. Then in her loneliness she gradually realized that she now had time to write a book. Both daughters were married and in homes of their own. Herbert was grown and teaching country school. So she began gathering material. It took two years for her to verify the historical background and interview many of the old inhabitants, to search through the library, and organize the plot of the story.

Her children were grateful that she had found something to occupy her time and attention. For one birthday her grandchildren gave her as presents a ream of typing paper, carbon paper, and a typewriter ribbon. Her hope was to sell the book to some well-known publisher so the story of Nauvoo could go to the world. But time after time the manuscript came back. Then she read that the *Saints' Herald* was sponsoring a contest for book-length stories, so she submitted her manuscript of *Joseph's City Beautiful.* It won first place. The book was published in 1939.

During the winter she lived with her children, but in summer she lived in her own home. Always she was writing. She and her grandchildren often sat on the banks of the Mississippi and watched the red-winged blackbirds and the squirrels. As they walked the streets of Nauvoo she told them about incidents in church history which had taken place there. She became a living tie connecting the Nauvoo of the past to the Nauvoo of the present. Hundreds of tourists bought copies of her book, and in this way her history of Nauvoo was carried into many areas.

She often read to her grandchildren and encouraged them to read while she listened. One of her daughters said, "Mother was interested in all subjects, and she made everything sound exciting. She was always encouraging others to read something she had enjoyed reading.

In 1943 at Kirtland Temple she was married to Robert H. Atkinson, a member of the church from Canada. They lived in St. Marys, Ontario, for a few years, but her desire to return to Iowa also became his desire, and they moved to Nauvoo.

She wrote a second book, *Land Shadowing With Wings,* published by Herald House. President F. M. Smith requested her to write it because he felt it would encourage people to read the Book of Mormon.

Robert and Mabel Atkinson had a happy life together. They attended church conferences and reunions, often traveling by jeep. He served as pastor of the Nauvoo Branch.

As her eyesight began to fail she found it difficult to read or write. She studied Braille and mastered the art of writing and reading it. She used a white cane when walking outside her home. She died on January 22, 1961, and was buried in Nauvoo.

Members of the church are indebted to Mabel Sanford Atkinson for preserving much of the history of the church in Nauvoo.

LOTTIE

CLARK

DIGGLE

The escape from the Indians was always vivid in her memory. Lottie was two years old at the time and her sister, Ida, was four. They lived in a log cabin in Prince Albert, Northwest Territory of Canada, and the year was 1885. Word came that the Indians were attacking the cabins of some of the settlers and that the Clarks should rush to the "manse house" which was a large building operated by the Hudson Bay Company. William Clark took a daughter under each arm. Mrs. Clark put a coat over her head but did not take time to put on her shoes. Through the snow they raced until they reached the house in safety. That night Mrs. Clark gave birth to a son.

103

Because there was no Indian attack in their immediate vicinity, they returned to their home. The father continued his work for the Hudson Bay Company. However, in March of 1885, hundreds of Indians rebelled against the loss of their lands, and the Canadian government sent soldiers from the east to fight. The Clarks lived near the trading post and were well protected.

Lottie, born July 3, 1883, was junior age when she suffered a severe siege of croup one bitterly cold winter. Her mother was away visiting at the time, but her father was home. Because a blizzard was occurring, it was impossible to go the five miles for a doctor. Lottie choked so much she could hardly breathe and death seemed imminent. Then her father knelt by her bed and prayed for help. She stopped choking and went quietly to sleep. That experience taught her that God was concerned about every individual.

She attended normal school and became a teacher. This meant she had to move to Regina. So many immigrants had moved there that it had become a large city. When the province of Saskatchewan was formed in 1905, Regina was made the capital city.

Lottie secured a teaching position and enjoyed the work. She joined a Protestant church in the community but she was not completely satisfied with its doctrine. Although she continued to attend services she still hoped to find a church like the one Christ established in New Testament times.

She became engaged to a young man, and prayed about her marriage, asking God for guidance. In a vision she was shown that the man she planned to marry would not make a good lifetime companion. In the same vision she saw another man who it was indicated would be a more dependable husband. Lottie did not know him.

In 1908 she obtained a teaching position in a community about fifteen miles from Saskatoon, Saskatchewan. She found a place to board with a pleasant couple. She was surprised when she saw their son, Carl Diggle; he was the young man she had seen in her vision. Most of the people in the community, including the couple with whom she was boarding, were members of the Reorganized Church. Services were held in the schoolhouse. Lottie told herself, "I will attend their meetings, but I will not believe their doctrine."

Lottie and Carl became engaged. One day he said, "My parents are members of the RLDS Church, and I plan to become a member also."

"That is fine," she told him. "I will never come between you and your church."

"Lottie, I want to be baptized, but I will wait until you are ready to be baptized also."

"That might be a long, long time—if ever," she answered.

They were married February 15, 1912. Carl opened a real estate office in Saskatoon, and soon after their marriage they bought a house that was to be their home for many years. Both of a religious nature, they dedicated their home to the Lord. Lottie attended a large church nearby and sang in the choir.

In 1914 a district conference of the Reorganized Church was held on the farm of Carl's parents. Lottie attended preaching services. Years later she wrote, "For two hours I sat on a plank bench in searing heat and listened to J. J. Cornish preach. His sermon was 'There is a God back of it all.' This was the first time I realized the church believed that revelation could be received now."

Lottie and Carl were baptized January 26, 1915, by T. J. Jordan, the district president. They returned to their home in Saskatoon and became active in the church's program. For the next eleven years services were held in their home.

Besides serving as district women's leader, Lottie directed the music, taught a class, and was in charge of branch publicity. The Saskatoon Branch was organized August 1, 1920, and Carl Diggle became the pastor.

Three children were born to the Diggles—a son, Marvin, and two daughters, Averil and Eileen. Besides being a busy mother and church worker, Lottie participated in many civic projects. She wrote in her autobiography:

It was late in 1923 that I became interested in first aid and home nursing. I became a member of the St. John Ambulance Brigade and practiced one evening weekly. Not long after I was invited to demonstrate to large classes of women and much to my surprise was later appointed official instructor for Saskatchewan. When war was declared in 1939 I was asked to take charge of all examinations in first aid.

Although I was active in the various offices of the Women's Christian Temperance Union, having at one time served six years as president of the local organization, as I grew older I confined my activities to provincial superintendent of drugs and narcotics, as program director and representative to the council of women.

Another challenging interest which began in the twenties but continued throughout my life was in the council of women which was a powerful organization from a provincial as well as national standpoint. In Saskatoon there were at times as many as sixty affiliated organizations. I was a member of the committee that organized the first home and school clubs in the city and had the privilege of being convenor of public health for several years; years later I was made convenor of laws.

After a number of home and school clubs were organized under the auspices of the council of women they amalgamated under a general council. I accepted the convenorship of education for five years, organizing classes for mothers of preschoolers, public school children, and teen-agers.

Between 1920 and 1940 church activities were given first place. I served many years as branch and district director of music, five years as children's supervisor, several as district women's leader, and also as supervisor of dramatics. An organization which interested me during the early thirties was the Children's Leaders' Council, members of which were representatives from various churches.

Sister Opal Price tells how her parents moved to Saskatoon when she was small. One of the first families to extend friendship to them was the Diggle family. As a young woman attending Nutana Collegiate, she lived in the Diggle home. During the summer of 1931 Lottie was sick, and Opal helped her with the three children. That same summer Opal was married to Ivor Price in a ceremony on the lawn of the Diggle house, with Carl officiating.

In 1934 Lottie was asked by the Department of Religious Education of the world church to teach a class in Saskatoon on the Book of Mormon, and in 1935 a class on the Doctrine and Covenants. Students in these classes could receive credits from the world church for the School of the Restoration in Independence, Missouri.

The Diggle children grew up, attended universities, married, and started homes of their own. Marvin became a member of the Royal Canadian Air Force. The house, once so full of life, became too quiet. When a high school student, Roderick Thompson, came to live with them, Lottie and Carl rejoiced.

In 1945 Opal and Ivor Price moved back to Saskatoon, now with a family of two small children. Their friendship with the Diggles continued. Carl was not well at this time, and his eyesight was failing. He did his Christmas shopping and purchased and wrapped a gift for Lottie. On Christmas Day he died. His body was taken to Independence, Missouri, for burial. Lottie and her sister-in-law, Mrs. Grace Beckman, also made the trip to Independence.

Before leaving, Lottie asked the Prices to move into her home and take care of it while she was away. When she came back she found that a third child had been born to them. Instead of returning to an empty house, she returned to a home with three lively children.

Lottie enjoyed writing and her material has been published in various church periodicals. Her first story appeared in *Stepping Stones*. "It was Leta B. Moriarty, associate editor," she wrote, "who inspired and encouraged me to do creative writing." In addition to her Herald House contributions, she wrote for the *District Leader,* a Canadian newsletter. She also served as historian of Saskatoon Branch and Saskatchewan District and as congregational publicity director.

One thing for which she will be warmly remembered is her work with the Senior Citizens Service Association of Saskatoon. This began about 1950 and continued until her death. For nine years she served as president of the board. Through the instigation of this association, the city council established a building where senior citizens could hold regular meetings. Of this work she wrote: "I look forward to a time when governments of cities, states, and provinces will establish such a center in every large community."

It was also in 1950 that she first attended World Conference. Again in 1952 she made the long trip from Saskatchewan to Missouri. Age did not alter her pleasing personality. She wrote, "This has been a good year with much joy, countless blessings, a few setbacks, an added ailment or two, a few friends who have passed on, but on the whole I have had more blessings. One blessing for which I am particularly grateful is the ability to write for the church. There is never a dull moment because of this God-given gift."

Lottie Diggle died November 17, 1967. Her children took her body from Saskatoon to Independence for burial beside their father's grave.

A friend wrote: "The threads of her life were woven into a fabric of faith, dedication, and service to make a beautiful garment of righteousness for others to admire and emulate." And her son said, "She did an amazing amount of work for the church and for her homeland, but most of all I remember her as a good mother."

ANNIE

BURTON

There was a loud noise, and the little house shook. Teen-age Annie Smith looked up in time to see the roof falling. She managed to free herself from the wreckage, but everything in the house was covered with the deep snow of the Canadian winter. The weight of it had caused the roof to collapse.

She called to the young couple who owned the house and for whom she was working. They answered, but their voices were muffled. The falling roof had blockaded them in their room. Annie could not move the heavy timbers but she knew the couple would freeze to death without heat, so she determined to go for help even though the temperature was 35 degrees below zero.

With determination she walked miles toward the nearest neighbor, praying as she plunged on. Her feet became so cold there was no feeling in them. By the time she reached the neighbor's house her feet were bleeding, and she could hardly speak.

Immediately some of the people of the household went to the rescue of the young couple. Annie Smith had saved their lives. "It is a miracle," the woman of the house said, "that you were able to walk this far in such weather."

Annie was born in Listoold, Ontario, Canada, May 25, 1884. She had a brother, Will, and two sisters, Minnie and Phoebe. The family lived alternately in Canada and the United States.

There were trials—such as the time in Manitoba when a storm destroyed all of their crops and damaged their home. That winter their only food was oatmeal porridge. And there was the time when the family worked hard to make a tent in which to live, only to have it destroyed by fire before they could use it.

As a child she was able to attend school for only a few months. She wanted an education, but woodlands and wild animals made it too dangerous for her to walk to school. At fourteen she drove a team of horses to help her father clear land.

When she was sixteen living in Manitoba, she attended a community picnic. There a young man, George Burton, was impressed with her and asked to meet her. Anne was pleased to become acquainted with him, for he was an outstanding youth. A few days later, a girl friend said, "Maybe he seems nice, but he is a Mormon.

There is a picture of Joseph Smith hanging in his home. You know all Mormons think Joseph Smith is a god and say their prayers to him. And George's parents are Mormons too."

When Annie's parents heard that her new friend was a Mormon they were annoyed. They thought all Latter Day Saints believed in polygamy. When George Burton asked Mr. Smith if he might visit Annie, the older man said, "No, and I do not want you coming to my house." George tried to explain about his religion, but Annie's father would not listen.

George Burton was a determined person. He returned to the Smith home and brought his mother along. Mr. and Mrs. Smith were considerate of her and invited the two into the house. George's mother explained the differences between the church in Utah and the Reorganized Church. She told them that the president of her church was Joseph Smith III, the son of Joseph Smith, Jr., and that the church believed in the one true God just as they did. Annie's father apologized and consented to let George "court" Annie.

George had three brothers, and all were members of the Reorganized Church. Their father was dead. Their stepfather, whom the boys loved, was also a member of the church.

When a missionary, Fred Gregory, came to the neighborhood and conducted church services, the Smith family attended, but when Annie wanted to be baptized, her father said, "No, you cannot. These Burtons are good people, but I am still not sure about their religion."

Annie accepted employment some distance from her

home. During the period of her employment it was difficult for her to contact George and her parents. When she returned home a surprise awaited her. Her parents and sisters had been baptized. Annie immediately united with the church on September 25, 1900, at Oak Nook, Manitoba.

She and George made plans to be married. The two mothers, now good friends, worked together planning the wedding, and Annie's aunt made a beautiful wedding dress. The marriage took place in the Smith home in February 1901. The father, who at one time would not let George Burton visit his house, was now happy to have him as a son-in-law.

George Burton owned land on which he had built a small log cabin. Before his marriage he had been busy working on this house. He replaced the sod roof with a shingled one. In the house were a table, cupboard, bed, six straight chairs, and a rocking chair—all homemade. This was the house into which Annie Burton moved as a bride. Poor in material wealth but rich in love and spiritual blessings, the couple found happiness here.

During the next few years a church was built near their home. Missionaries from eastern Canada and the United States often stayed in the home of Annie and George Burton, A son, Fred, and a daughter, Sadie, were born to the Burtons. As much as possible the family attended church, in winter traveling by horse-drawn sleigh.

Then in 1905 a change came. People in eastern Canada were moving and a railroad was being built to the coast. The Burtons and Smiths planned to move into this "newer" country.

The two families rented two railroad cars and loaded their belongings into them. Annie's husband and brother left on this same train. Ten days later, Annie, her children, her sisters, and her parents left on another train. The train went through dense woods and wide, unkept prairies. They slept in their seats, and ate the lunches they had brought. Eventually the train stopped at a small town called Elbow. Here Annie discovered that her husband and brother had gone farther west. The railroad man explained, "I let them go to the end of the line because they were looking after your freight, but I can't let you folks go any farther than Elbow. The railroad beyond here is not ready for passenger service." Annie reasoned with the man. "All right," the man agreed, "I'll let you go, but you must sign a paper for me saying that if any of you are killed or injured, I am not to blame. And since there is no passenger car you will all have to ride in the caboose." Annie, her mother, and sisters became the first white women to move to this part of Western Canada.

At first they lived in a place called North Battlefield. Here they became acquainted with Indians, and on one occasion an Indian youth saved Annie and Phoebe from being molested by four white men. Then they moved to Ribstone, Alberta, securing their land directly from the government. They were the first white people to settle in that area. They selected fertile land along the Ribstone Creek and built log cabins.

That fall more settlers came. Among them were George's parents and his brothers, Anson and Herbert. Eventually Annie's sister, Minnie, married Herbert Burton. "Now," joked Annie, "my sister is my sister-in-law."

Ribstone became a community. Because Annie and Phoebe desired a church missionary to visit the community they wrote a letter to the *Herald* telling about the agricultural wealth of the country and asking other church members to move to Alberta.

The W. J. Levitt family of Michigan came first. Among others who came later was Charlie Waite, also of Michigan, and Annie's sister, Phoebe, became his bride. So many people came that the villages of Edgerton and Artland were founded, and each village was a branch of the church. All this happened because two women wrote a letter to the *Herald.*

In the years that followed, prominent church people visited these communities. It was a thrilling experience when President F. M. Smith came to Ribstone. In 1913 a church was built on the farm of George and Annie Burton. Once when Missionary J. J. Cornish was visiting in their home, he said to Annie, "Sister, you have done much for the Lord in kingdom building. You have caused branches of the church to be built, and you have continued to try to keep them growing."

Whenever possible Annie tried to get more education. She liked to read, and worked at becoming proficient. She saw that her children attended school. Two more daughters, Belle and Bessie, and a son, George, were born to the Burtons.

Annie served for years as secretary of Ribstone Branch and also as women's leader. She kept in touch with branch members who lived too far away to attend services regularly. She and her children would travel by

115

wagon—drawn by a team of horses or a yoke of oxen—to visit them. In some areas there were no roads, only trails across fields.

She delighted in having missionaries stay in her home, and wanted the children to hear the stories of their experiences. The children grew up, married, and moved into homes of their own. In 1940 Annie and George sold their farm and moved to Ribstone, which had become a city of considerable size. Later they moved to Wainright and lived in an apartment in the home of a daughter and her husband.

At the age of eighty-seven George died. Because it became increasingly difficult for her to hear, Annie avoided attending church until she was spoken to under divine inspiration: "It is my will that you come to prayer meetings even though you cannot hear, and that you seek to minister to my people here by your presence, also by your prayers and testimonies. Seek to be humble and full of love. If you will do this I will continue to bless you."

When Missionary Eric Rowe was appointed to this section of Canada, he went to visit Annie. Before he left, they knelt in prayer. In a letter telling about the experience, Annie wrote, "I was facing into the corner and couldn't see him, but I could hear distinctly every word he said. I felt that I was surrounded by a bright light. It seemed to be everywhere. I wanted to see if it surrounded him too, but I hesitated to move for fear it would leave." When she saw Elder Rowe days later at church he told her that he had also witnessed the heavenly light.

Annie Burton died January 12, 1969, at Wainwright,

Alberta. She had been a woman with little opportunity for education or material gain, but she had lived a life that permitted God to bless her home with his Spirit.

ANNA

JOHANSSON

The young Swedish woman held in her hands a copy of the *Saints' Herald* printed in English. She read the words slowly for she was mastering a language foreign to her. Then she smiled at the church elders who had brought the copy of the church paper to her.

"What does it say, Sister Johansson?" they asked. Anna Johansson translated the English into Swedish.

"Thank you for bringing us this message," one of them said. "We appreciate your going to the trouble to learn the English language. Because of your efforts, we are able to understand the church papers and the messages sent from church headquarters in Independence, Missouri."

This brought joy to the heart of Sister Anna. She was not healthy, and there seemed so little she could do to serve the church.

Presiding Patriarch Roy A. Cheville wrote about his visit to her: "She resolved to do something to assist the church in her country. She struggled alone to read English and thereby became the means of communication between the few members in Sweden and the church in America. She took the *Herald* and relayed the news to her people. The day we were in her room at the rest home, a copy of the *Herald* lay on her table. She was worthy of the benediction we prayed on leaving. 'Little Anna' in her wheelchair has been a stay to our very few members in Sweden."

Anna and her twin brother, August, were born January 8, 1896, in Sodermanland, Sweden. August was a strong, healthy baby. Anna was small and frail. The Johansson home with its family of ten children was about thirty-five miles south of Stockholm.

As Anna grew older, she found that the bones in her body were so weak they often broke, especially those in her legs. August attended the public school, but Anna had to go to a home in Stockholm for crippled children. There she attended a special school. In addition to an academic education she learned needlecraft—embroidery, knitting, crocheting, tatting, and lace making. Her hands became stronger as she developed skills in these crafts.

She had a keen intellect, enjoyed people, and made friends easily. She became known to relatives and friends as "Little Anna." Her older brother, Oscar, went to Stockholm to work. He was kind to Anna, and a close relationship developed between them. Anna loved Oscar dearly.

During the summers she would go home where she could help some with household tasks. There was a beautiful lake near her home, and she enjoyed going for boat rides. If careful, she was able to pick berries.

As she grew older she became a seamstress and supported herself at this trade. Frequently she made bridal gowns and dresses, but she was best known for her knitting, embroidery, and crocheting.

At this time the Church of Jesus Christ of Latter-day Saints had missionaries in Sweden. Oscar became convinced that they were preaching the truth and was baptized in 1900. He told Anna about the church, but she did not join.

The following year he moved to Salt Lake City in Utah. Anna and her parents received letters from him telling about his work and his church and the new country in which he was living. Then the letters began to say he was no longer happy with his church. In 1904 he was baptized a member of the Reorganized Church of Jesus Christ of Latter Day Saints and wrote enthusiastically to Anna about this church. A few years later he wrote that he had married Maria Swenson who had also come from Sweden. He was now spelling his name Johnson instead of Johansson.

In 1910 Oscar and his wife visited Sweden. He was serving as a missionary. Anna rejoiced at seeing her brother again and loved her new sister-in-law. In 1913 Oscar and Maria returned to the United States. Anna continued to live with her parents and sell needlework. All her brothers and sisters married. Her twin brother moved to the United States.

She was twenty-four years old when Oscar again returned to Sweden. With him came his wife and two small daughters. Anna had not united with the church her brother represented, but she was interested. Then, in 1920, she began to study tracts available in the Swedish language. She too desired to learn English so she could read the *Herald* and other church literature printed in the United States. Every winter Anna lived in the home of her brother and sister-in-law. When another daughter was born to them, Anna loved her and cared for her as much as possible. The three little girls were dear to her.

Years later her oldest niece wrote of her: "When Mother and Dad were away serving the church in other parts of Sweden, Aunt Anna was left in charge of our house. She was a second mother to us. We loved her. Through the years I have treasured the memory of the times we spent together. I feel I am a much better person for having known and loved my little Aunt Anna."

In 1923 Anna was baptized in a lake near Stockholm by her brother. She wanted to be of service to the church and wondered what she could do. When she made her desire a subject of prayer, God guided her in her decision. She would master the English language so she could be a translator for her paper. She spent much time studying. Oscar and Maria helped her until their return to the States in 1927. They corresponded often, and in 1932 the sad news came that Maria had died as the result of an automobile accident.

James Everett, former missionary to the Scandinavian countries, wrote of Anna: "When the depression years hit the church, it was unfortunately necessary to withdraw the appointee missionaries from Sweden. This measure was to be only temporary, but the missionary absence stretched out for years. During this time Sister Anna's knowledge of English grew in importance; not only was she able to supply herself with news from and about the world church but at times she was the only communication channel between the world church and the local Swedish-speaking priesthood who, in turn, could inform the rest of the church members concerning news and doctrine. In this area alone it is not exaggeration to say that 'Little Anna' made a contribution equal to any in the history of the Swedish mission. From 1927 to 1953 during which time she maintained her own home, it was the one place that always had room for visiting ministry from America or for the appointees from neighboring Norway. She served as the interpreter at cottage meetings and other small, informal groups. She always subscribed to the church periodicals and paid her tithing."

Another appointee, Donald D. Landon, wrote about her in the *Herald*: "Her twisted and pain-wracked body has been a burden heavy enough to fill the eyes and depress the soul of the most courageous. But every time I visited her I was made aware of the fact that the gospel had brought a joy into her life which was impervious even to her ill health. She was an assured person. The love of God was more real to her than her twisted hands. Her fellowship with her Redeemer was experienced more deeply than the pain of her tortured back.

122

Her inner resource of joy could never be touched by the passing things of this world, including handicap and pain."

In 1953 Sister Johansson moved into a rest home for the aged. It was now necessary for her to use a hearing aid and to wear strong glasses. She was confined to a wheelchair. Her right arm became practically paralyzed. In order to continue her correspondence with church friends she learned to write with her left hand. At this age and under such trying conditions, some people would have stopped trying and would have lost interest altogether.

It was this bright personality that impressed Rosamond Smith, wife of President W. Wallace Smith, when the Smiths visited her. In a talk given at a women's institute Sister Smith said, "She brings cheer to all who come in contact with her. She is one of the sweetest people I have ever met in my life. When a person who has been visiting her leaves, she always waves good-by. When President Smith and I left, she sat in her wheelchair and waved to us with a handkerchief. We looked back as much as we could. She continued to wave farewell. What a wonderful soul she has." In a letter printed to the *Herald* she wrote:

As I cannot write a personal letter to each one of you, I will try to reach you through the columns of the *Herald*. I want to thank all of you for the good spiritual letters which we are receiving regularly twice a month from the missionaries who have labored more than words can express; they bring to us cheer and encouragement. In the absence of a missionary in Scandinavia, we are grateful to President Smith for his suggestion that former missionaries to these countries write a circular letter twice a month to be sent to all of the families of Saints here.

I still believe that this church is the best one on earth, and I am constantly asking God to bless his children and his servants with the Spirit of Christ that his kingdom may come on earth as it is in heaven. Please remember us in your prayers. For the Saints in Sweden, by a sister in gospel bonds, Anna Johansson.

Anna died July 1, 1968, but she will never be forgotten by the church people in Sweden.

ANNA

SOFKE

Anna Frank hummed softly to herself as she picked the mushrooms that grew in the woods near her home in Germany. It was early morning, and the dew still glistened on leaves and grass. She picked the mushrooms and took them immediately into the village nearby to sell to the housewives. This was the way she earned money.

Anna was born September 27, 1889, in Pontwitz, Germany. Her father was a devout Catholic, her mother a Protestant. Both parents and the four children attended the Catholic church.

After she completed eight years of grade school she served an apprenticeship as a cook in an officers mess hall in the German army. For this she received a small salary as well as her training. She learned how to prepare gourmet dishes and enjoyed serving large dinners prepared for special occasions.

After completing her apprenticeship she worked as a cook in the homes of wealthy people. Then came World War I, and Germany was in turmoil. Instead of cooking, Anna worked as a section controller for the German Railway. There she met Karl Sofke, a young man who belonged to the same Protestant church her mother did.

Anna and Karl were married in April 1919. During the first ten years of their married life they lived in the village near her parents. Then Karl transferred to Ober-Stradam, and Anna and the children joined him. Here they came in contact with the Reorganized Church.

Every day Anna and a woman from whom she bought the local newspaper had long conversations about religion and conditions following the war. Anna was amazed at how wise the woman was and how much she knew about the Bible and Christ. The woman—a Latter Day Saint—invited Anna Sofke to attend the Bible class of which she was a member.

Anna and her stepdaughter, Erna, began attending classes. After she had been there several times, Karl objected. "You should not listen to these other speakers. They tell falsehoods," he would say. But by this time Anna was convinced that the Reorganized Church was true, and she continued to attend the classes and to take the children with her.

Another son, Georg, was born to the Sofkes in 1931, and Anna became very ill. The doctor told Karl that she might die. When Anna expressed the desire to be baptized, Karl said, "Well, go ahead and do it if you feel strong enough."

That was all the encouragement she needed. On November 1, 1931, she was baptized at Wartenberg. After that she felt stronger.

Church tracts had been printed in the German language, and copies of these were brought to the Sofke home. Four months after Anna's baptism, Erna joined the church.

The local missionary Johann Smolny (John Smolney) held a series of meetings. Anna asked Karl to attend these with her, and he agreed. As he listened to Brother Smolny he became impressed with the truthfulness of the message. He was baptized also.

In her autobiography, Anna Sofke wrote, "Our marriage, which had always been a good one, was now complete through our common faith. My husband was soon called to the office of teacher."

In 1938 Karl Sofke became extremely ill. His last words to her before his death were, "Hold fast to that which you have and try to bring the children up in faith."

Then came difficult times. The two oldest daughters married and established homes of their own. Alfred, eighteen, had finished his apprenticeship at a trade and was able to help support the family. Georg was only seven. Anna cleaned houses, did washing, ironing, and cooking. And she saw to it that her children attended church regularly. There was no RLDS group in the village where they lived, so every Sunday they walked five miles to services and five miles home.

Georg, who later became a missionary for the church, wrote about this experience: "I still remember a Communion service followed by a prayer and testimony meeting. I dedicated my life to God and expressed a desire to serve him. Later that afternoon as the pastor was taking us home with his horse and sleigh (it had snowed so much that we couldn't walk home), he said that one day my desire would be fulfilled. That was in 1942. I have asked myself often since then what it was that drew me to those meetings. Most of the boys at school went to the Hitler Youth meetings. Later it was forced upon all. Was it the quality of the lives of the church members which drew me? Was it their fellowship? They believed and thought differently than the majority. I believe now that I was moved by the Spirit of God in those young years."

War came again to Germany. Anna's oldest son was killed. Seventeen-year-old Gerhard was drafted and sent into battle against the Russians. Her daughter Gertrud found employment in another village. Citizens of the town where Anna lived often talked about what they would do if the Russian army came. Then one very cold day in January 1945 a messenger stopped at every door to warn the people that the Russians were approaching, and the people must leave immediately. Anna and Georg, taking only limited clothing and food, made their escape.

Of this Georg writes: "We were forced to leave home in the wake of the fast approaching Red Army. My mother and I walked about five hundred miles in two months toward the west. The farther we were away from home, the worse it became. All side roads . . . for the main roads had to be left free for the German Army ... were jammed with fleeing, freezing, starving people. Twice we found ourselves at the Russian-German front and barely escaped death. Once as we had been without food for several days, I didn't want to go any farther. I sat down by the side of the road and cried. My mother could give me nothing, but said: "God will not leave us alone." I did go on and decided for the first time in my life to beg for bread. I'll never forget the first house into which I went ... as I will never forget many, many other things on this long, desperate trip." They continued the march for six weeks during winter weather. Their shoes wore thin, and their exposed feet left spots of blood on the snow. They slept in vacant buildings or in wooded areas. Births and deaths occurred along the way.

Georg's account of the experience ends with this paragraph: "The route of escape led us through Czechoslovakia up to the German border of Bavaria. This is where we were when the war ended. Unfortunately we couldn't go over into Bavaria immediately after the war, for we were not allowed to leave Czechoslovakia. It was not until a night in March 1946 that my mother and I were finally able to slip across the border into Germany. After we had been in several refugee camps we settled in the village of Geinsenfeld in Bavaria. I was fourteen."

Gerhard was undernourished and weak after spending weeks in a Russian prison camp. Following his release at the close of the war he found where his mother and Georg were living and traveled to the village in Bavaria to be with them.

Gerhard and Georg found work with the railroad, just

129

as their father had years before. Anna also found employment again. Every Sunday she and her two sons traveled forty miles by train and by foot to the village of Augsburg to attend services of the Reorganized Church. Although the sorrows of the war were still a heavy burden on her heart, Anna enjoyed being with the Saints again.

When her sons grew older, they married women who were Catholics; both wives were eventually baptized into the Reorganized Church. Anna loved her daughters-in-law and delighted in telling them about her conversion.

In 1950, when she was sixty years old, Anna received a government pension. This meant she no longer had to work so hard. Today she lives alone in an apartment in Offenbach. Her children and grandchildren visit her frequently. She is active in church work and every year attends the mission conference in Hannover. Her son Gerhard and his family live three blocks away. He served as pastor of the local congregation. On Easter Sunday of 1969 he was ordained a patriarch.

A few miles away lives Georg and his family. In 1963 he was made a church appointee. Both he and his wife are diligent workers for the church.

Erna and her children are only a few miles away also. Her husband was killed in the war. Gertrud and her husband, who is in the priesthood, and their children live near. Another daughter, Hedel, and her husband and family live in Bavaria.

Saints in Germany call Anna "Oma" (grandmother). In a way, she might be called the grandmother of the church in Germany. There were many times in her life when it might have been easy to have forgotten the church, but she did not. And her faith, devotion, and strength have been passed on to others.

ALICE

LEWIS

H ow old was she?" asked a friend. "Ninety-seven," the daughter of the woman answered.

"If she could have lived only three more years she would have been one hundred," said the friend, "and then she would have received a letter from the Queen of England."

"She was tired and not well," explained the daughter. "She said she would rather go on into the next world than suffer three years more in this one."

They were talking about Alice Ann Lewis who died in her native land of Australia, July 22, 1964. She was born November 26, 1866, at Waratah, New South Wales, and at the age of nine moved with her family to

Wallsend. Her father, Thomas Gregory, a good man, worked in the coal mines. He often said, "I started to work in the mines of England when I was just six years old. Hour after hour I held the candle for my father so he could see to dig coal. I never went to school a day in my whole life, but my children are going to be educated." Alice's mother agreed that the children should receive an education.

Alice, her five sisters, and one brother attended public school a short distance from their home. The headmaster was such a stern, unpleasant person that few students enjoyed school or learned the value of study.

In 1874 when Alice was seven years old, two missionaries, Charles W. Wandell and Glaud Rodger, journeyed from the United States to Australia to preach the restored gospel. At one time Brother Wandell had been a missionary for the Church of Jesus Christ of Latter-day Saints, and he brought with him the addresses of a Brother Marriott in Waratah and Thomas Gregory of Wallsend. Thomas also had joined the Church of Jesus Christ of Latter-day Saints while still a young man in England. When he learned that it was not the same as the original church, he no longer attended it faithfully. Now that two missionaries from the Reorganized Church were preaching near his home he decided to investigate.

Alice and her sister Rachel went with their father to these meetings. Because they were too poor to own a horse, they walked the six miles to Waratah and then home again; the missionaries also walked the six miles to visit in the Gregory home. Evenings when the family sat before the fireplace, the Gregory children listened with sincere interest to the missionary accounts of the greatness of God and the restored gospel. They also heard their father and Brother Wandell discuss the differences between the two churches.

Alice's parents became members of the Reorganized Church, and she was baptized January 15, 1876. When a branch was organized at Waratah, Thomas Gregory was made pastor. It was later moved to Wallsend.

Alice attended the local school until she was fourteen; in those days in New South Wales this was considered a rather good education for a woman. After leaving school, she began doing professional sewing for other people. The money she earned in this manner helped her father support the family.

In prophecy she was told that she would some day visit the church headquarters in Independence, Missouri. She could not understand how she would ever have an opportunity to make such a long trip, but she thought about it as she busied herself with her sewing.

A few days before Christmas of 1884 Missionary Joseph Burton, his wife Emma, and their daughter Addie arrived in Australia. They lived at Wallsend much of the time, and Alice and Addie became the best of friends. Addie and her mother also supported themselves by sewing for other people. Many times the three women would sit together sewing and Emma would tell about life in Canada, the United States, and Tahiti.

Alice was married in 1890 to George Lewis, a member of the church. He was a young businessman with a good education. They established their home in Wallsend. Their first child, a daughter, was named Addie in honor of Addie Burton.

For fourteen years George Lewis was business manager for an organization; then he opened a store of his own. Eight children were born to the Lewises—six girls and two boys. All were taught to serve the church.

Saints in Wallsend wanted to erect a church building but they did not have sufficient funds. In 1896 Alice's parents bought another house, moved into it, and let the Saints meet in their former house. Years later a church was built. In 1901 Alexander H. Smith, son of Emma and Joseph Smith, Jr., went to Australia. In December of that year Alice and George met him. When he first saw George he said, "This is the man I have been sent to ordain a bishop." Then George became the first bishop of the church in Australia. This meant that he had to travel and be away from home. The family worked harder in the store. Alice explained, "We want the business to be so well organized that the children and I can manage it while George is gone."

The sorrows of World War I were felt in Australia. When she was a grown woman Alice's daughter Lily Ley wrote of her mother: "During the first World War mother was a tireless worker. She served in the Red Cross and in the Benevolent Society. Our old sewing machine went constantly while she made comforters and pajamas for soldiers."

The Benevolent Society was established for the needy people of New South Wales. Alice Lewis and Mrs. Estell, the wife of a member of Parliament, visited the home of every person who applied for help; they arranged to have necessary food and clothing sent to their homes. Most of these people were miners, and because the mines were frequently closed for long periods of time workers' families had no support.

Many of the miners could not pay their bills at the Lewis store. Generous Alice and George let them charge more and more things to their accounts, but since the Lewises did not receive payment from the customers, they could not pay their creditors. Their business failed, and the store had to be closed.

In 1924 their son George G. Lewis went to the United States to attend Graceland. He had been employed by the Australian government. In one of his letters a few years later he wrote that he had been ordained an elder. Alice's desire to attend World Conference came true in 1930. She traveled in a group of sixteen Saints under the leadership of Elder W. J. Haworth, manager of the Standard Publishing House in Australia and president of New South Wales District. A delegation of thirty-two church members met the Australian Saints. The travelers were taken by cars on a sight-seeing tour of Kansas City and visited the home of President F. M. Smith. At the Laurel Club in the Auditorium they were served a lunch. Following this, Alice was among those asked to make brief remarks.

While in Missouri she visited Addie Burton who was now married and living in Independence. Toward the end of her visit Alice was injured in an auto accident and had to spend several days in the Independence Sanitarium and Hospital. She recuperated in time to return home with the group of Australian Saints.

She had been home only a few months when George died suddenly from a stroke. In New South Wales it is the custom that mourners at a funeral walk, not ride, behind the casket. Because the Lewises had many friends the procession for George included church people, business associates, miners, and Chinese merchants.

Following the death of her husband, Alice closed her home. She and her two youngest children, Sadie and Neil, moved to Hamilton to live with Lily and Harry Ley. Alice helped care for the house and did a lot of sewing. She also grew flowers and shared them with friends.

A letter from her son George in 1929 brought the happy news that he had been married on September 19 to Edith Olene Woods. In another letter in 1932 he wrote of his ordination to the office of apostle on April 15. That same year he and his wife went to Australia. They remained there until 1938. Edith Lewis says of her mother-in-law, "She was always on hand when I needed help. I wish every woman could have a mother-in-law like mine."

Gwen Roberts, a granddaughter, remembered Alice Lewis only as an elderly woman: "Every year she would spend a few weeks in our home, and during that time she would make our school clothes. What pretty dresses she could make . . . and she was fun! She would let her long white hair hang around her face when we were getting ready to go to bed and would play that she was Mrs. Santa Claus. We all loved her."

During her later years when her health began to fail she was cared for by her daughter, Lily, assisted by friends and neighbors. In 1960, when Lily and Harry Ley left for World Conference in Independence, Alice went to live with her daughter Sadie.

Following her death, Leona Burdekin, a faithful worker in the department of women in Australia, said, "She was respected by hundreds of people and represented the church to many of them. She was an example to all our church women in Australia."

EMERE

MERVIN

In 1948 a group of Tahitians traveled from French Polynesia to Independence, Missouri, to attend World Conference. Among them were Elder and Sister John Mervin.

Emere Mervin was the first Tahitian woman of the church to make this journey. As she sat in the Auditorium, she thought about the events that had led up to this moment.

In Tahiti there is always the rhythmic sound of ocean waves splashing the shore and the pleasant sight of flowers and green trees. Most of the island men work at jobs connected with collecting pearl shell or preparing copra from coconuts. Both products are shipped to other countries.

Emere was born in 1905 at the village of Panau on the island of Kaukura. Her father, Pori Bellais, was a leader on the island. He was also an elder in the Reorganized Church and pastor of Kaukura Branch. Her mother was the first leader of the department of women in Kaukura.

Emere had a happy childhood. One of the subjects she studied in public school was French. (Tahiti is under the rule of France.) The native Tahitian language was spoken in her home.

Because her parents were active church members she learned to have great respect for the Restoration. Her mother often told her about the missionaries who had served in the islands and of the visit in November 1901 of Alexander Smith, a son of Joseph and Emma, who was a member of the First Presidency. As Emere listened she wondered if she would ever have a chance to see a member of the Presidency.

She was baptized in the ocean near Panau by Missionary J. Charles May in November 1913, when she was eight years old. The following year a chapel was built on the island of Kaukura. Emere enjoyed watching this building being erected. She knew it would be a place where the Tahitian Saints could worship and learn.

At the age of thirteen Emere attended school in Papeete. This meant that she had to be away from home much of the time, but she was growing older and more independent.

When Emere was eighteen she became interested in a handsome young man, John Tihoni Mervin. He proposed marriage to Emere, but because he was not a member of the church she refused. Even though he promised to be baptized after they were married, Emere still said, "No."

John left Kaukura and went to work on the island of Apataki. When he was away an elder of the church said to Emere. "I have had a dream about Tihoni, and it was a good dream. I saw him and an elder who lives on Apataki. They were in a canoe together. The canoe capsized and the two men went into the water and then swam to shore together. This means that Tihoni has been baptized."

Several days later John returned to Kaukura, and he had been baptized. He and Emere were married in Kaukura in 1922. At their wedding they promised to give their lives in service and to dedicate their home to God. Following their marriage, they moved to Papeete and became members of Tarona Branch. John was ordained an elder and gave outstanding ministry. For ten years Emere served as the women's leader of the branch.

Two of the six children born to the Mervins died while young. In their place two nieces were adopted.

When Brother and Sister Mervin visited Independence in 1948, they both spoke to the Conference. After extending greetings from the French Polynesian Saints Sister Mervin said, "It is indeed a pleasure for me to meet here in this, the Center Place, with the good women of the church. The good word that has been taught by our excellent leader of the women shall remain with me and when I return to the islands I shall share it with the women there. I shall also carry the love of the people at this General Conference back to Tahiti. We shall not forget how we have been assisted in our stay here. May the Lord continue to bless all of us in the name of Jesus Christ."

In 1950 President Israel A. Smith and Bishop Mark Siegfried visited the Mervin home in Tahiti. President W. Wallace Smith and his wife, Rosamond, visited Tahiti in 1961. Emere and the other women were delighted to have Rosamond Smith with them. This was the first time that the wife of a president of the church had visited Tahiti.

In 1964 Emere sent a letter to Kathryn Westwood, director of the Department of Women. In it she said, "I write to you in regard to the work which I am doing here as district women's leader in Tahiti. I am very pleased to hold this office and do what I am able to do."

Although her husband was taken from her by death, Emere's faith remained firm. She continued to live in Tahiti among her family and friends, and she continues to serve God and mankind as best she can.

Terii Maru Aa, a young Tahitian woman who is also doing much good for the church, writes of Sister Mervin, "She is like a real mother to many of us in the islands."

PAULINE

ARNSON

On a cold day in December 1965, an older woman, using a cane, made her way slowly across the parking lot behind the Auditorium. Three young women hurrying across the same parking lot smiled at her as they passed. She nodded cheerfully and smiled back. They hurried on, not realizing that they had passed a woman who had influenced not only their lives but the lives of many other members of the church. She was Mrs. Shankland Arnson who, for over twenty years, had served as director of the Department of Women for the World Church.

Pauline James was born February 21, 1898, in Independence, Missouri, to Orville and Belle Robinson

James. She was baptized on April 22, 1906, in the Stone Church Annex. When the family lived in Oklahoma, she would travel with her parents to the home of her grandparents, John and Jane Robinson, in Independence to attend Conference. She found pleasure in going with her cousins and uncles and aunts to business sessions in the big Stone Church, but most of all she liked seeing her mother serve as the official stenographer at World Conferences.

Music, which was to play a prominent part in her life, became precious to her during childhood. Because both her parents were musically inclined, she learned to sing at an early age. She studied piano, violin, and voice.

When Pauline was ready to enter high school, the James family made a trip to Europe. She and her brother, under their mother's tutelage, kept up their schoolwork so they could be graduated with their friends. Pauline continued her education at high schools in Independence and Kansas City, Missouri, and was graduated in 1916.

The summer she was eighteen the family spent a few weeks vacation in Colorado. While she was filing her nails one day the file suddenly slipped and pierced her left eye. She was rushed to the office of an ophthalmologist who said, "The fluid has been drained from that eye. I doubt if she will ever see out of it again." He dressed the eye and gave her pills to take home, assuring her she would need them because the pain would be severe. That evening her parents drove several miles to take her to a church missionary, J. Charles May, for administration. The next morning when Mrs. James was changing the dressing, Pauline said, "Mamma, you have

144

on a pink dress. I can see it." When the doctor examined her, he was amazed at the improvement. The vision in her left eye was a little blurred the rest of her life, but she could see.

Following high school she attended school in Washington, D.C., and Teachers College at Emporia, Kansas. She accompanied her parents on several more trips to Europe and studied voice in France. She learned to speak French so proficiently that few could tell it was not her native tongue.

Her parents constantly taught her, "The person who has the opportunity to receive special education must never consider himself superior to those who do not have the same opportunity but he must dedicate himself to sharing what he knows with the less fortunate." This became a guiding motto in Pauline's life.

Music continued to be one of her major interests. She was a charter member of the Independence Music Club which was organized in 1920 and continued to be active in that organization. For six years she was a featured singer on a Kansas City radio station. Seven times she was the soloist for the Kansas City Messiah Choir which performed in the Music Hall. She was also an instructor of music at the Independence high school.

Pauline became interested in the church's program for women, and she was asked to serve on the executive committee for the World Church Women's Department in 1922. This marked the beginning of her years of dedicated service in women's work.

On April 30, 1927, she married Shankland S. Arnson. At the time he was not a member of the church but he was baptized six years later and eventually became a member of the priesthood. He also served as a member of the Herald House Board of Publication.

In 1930 the Arnsons moved to a home in the Englewood area. Although Pauline had wanted to attend Stone Church, her husband convinced her that they should support the Englewood congregation which at that time met in a basement. "Our services are needed there," he said, "and what good is our faith if we cannot serve?" When they began attending Englewood, she was immediately asked to take charge of the choir. She did, and many people had the pleasure of singing under her guidance.

At one time the General Department of Women was a section of the Department of Religious Education. President F. M. Smith was not satisfied with this arrangement and insisted that the women of the church should have their own department and that women should be in charge of it. He selected Pauline as the woman to organize and direct the work of the new Department of Women. When he told her his plans she said, "I don't know how to do this. Music is my talent."

He insisted, "You have more than one talent. Are you going to be satisfied to use just one?" "No," she said, "but I must think about this before I give you an answer."

Pauline went to her aunt, Mrs. Jennie Yingling, to talk about the assignment. "I know so little about the church's program for women," she said. Sister Yingling, who had worked with Pauline on the executive council for women, assured her that she had been selected for the purpose of organizing and improving the program, not for continuing with the past program. "You know the importance of giving service to the church," she said. "You have training and experience in organizing your life. You can move with assurity. You have had the opportunity of training in refined cultures, and you know any education you have is not for yourself alone but for sharing with others."

This was much the same as her mother had written in a letter to her: "You are in possession of culture, talent, refinement, purity, honesty, and above all you have a deep spiritual nature that speaks well for all those with whom you come in contact."

And so Pauline James Arnson, a woman who could have lived a life of leisure, agreed to devote herself to the women of the church. A council of eight women from Missouri and eight from outside the state were selected to assist her. The work she began in January 1934 lasted over two decades. Because of the sickness of her mother she could give little time to this assignment at first but Sister James died April 5, 1935.

Because no office space was allotted to the Department of Women in the Auditorium building, Pauline set up an office in her home. "I had to learn to type and keep records," she said. "We held council meetings around our dining room table." Brother Arnson paid the bills for supplies and postage until 1936 when the church began providing stationery and postage for correspondence. But there was no budget for the department, and the women could not be sure of getting needed supplies.

In 1938 the Department of Women was given office space in the Auditorium. Pauline brought furniture from her home, as did the other women; they also constructed bookcases and collected reference books for an office library.

Her job demanded more and more of her time, leaving little for the music she so loved. She taught classes, gave talks, planned goals for the department, arranged programs, and wrote articles. Many times she traveled alone to assignments in other cities. On these trips she gave not only advice but ministry. Evelyn Velt, one of her associates, said, "She always attempted to make the average woman feel important. She insisted that work sincerely done, by any woman, was of value. At classes where she taught and places where she lectured, she would seek out unskilled and untrained women with whom to visit. She would say, 'I just might be of help to them.' "

In September 1938 a thousand copies of the *Handbook for the Work of the Women of the Church* was published. Women were so eager for this information that the entire supply was purchased and more had to be printed immediately. Pamphlets, tracts, and study courses were written for women by authors selected by Sister Arnson, and articles of special interest to women were printed in the *Herald*.

Never during her years of service did Pauline receive monetary payment. She would do her housework and then go to the office the remainder of the day. When she retired in 1954 she did not stop serving the women of the church. For six more years she was a member of the General Council of Women, doing more writing, making speeches, serving on committees, traveling to institutes, and teaching at reunions.

Her husband, who had become an evangelist, died

June 2, 1962. After his death, she continued to live in their home in Kansas City, Missouri. Six months later her brother died as the result of an accident.

Because of her ability to speak and write French, she was asked to do translations to be used by the church in Tahiti. She was not well, and this was a service she could give in her own home.

Pauline Arnson died February 8, 1966. That same year the Pauline James Arnson Memorial Library was established by Kathryn Westwood who had become the director of the Department of Women. The library is part of the headquarters offices of the General Department of Women and consists of both a lending and a reference library.

Mary Moats, who served as a member of the Council of Women under Pauline, wrote of her: "An outstanding example of the acceptance of responsibility is found in the life of Pauline Arnson. With her acceptance, she brought all her gracious charm and effort into this new work. Because she was willing to develop previously unused talents, the department was enriched, and she found joy of service in an unlimited field."

ADAH

WEBB

Church author Leona Hands has written: "The best way to describe Adah Webb is to say that she is an angel with a crutch." Hundreds of people would agree with this. Sister Webb has never had the opportunity to travel, but her words of wisdom and her acts of love have been taken by other people to other lands.

Adah was born June 29, 1885, in Buhl Center, Michigan, the daughter of Robert and Ada Webb. She had seven older brothers and sisters. Her father's work frequently took him away from the home for several weeks at a time. Once while he was away, two missionaries—Robert and John Grant—held services near the Webb home. Mrs. Webb and the children attended.

She was convinced of the truthfulness of the gospel and was baptized. When Robert came home and discovered this he was extremely angry.

At an early age Adah developed an urge to read and study. The family Bible seemed almost as big as she was, but she would carry it around while her mother was doing the housework and ask, "What's this word?" Her parents and older brothers and sisters encouraged her interest.

When she was eleven the Webb family moved to Port Huron, Michigan. On June 16, 1907, she was baptized in Lake Huron by Elder Charles C. Whitford. As she grew older she worked in a store as a clerk. She had a cheerful disposition and could usually provide a quick, humorous answer to problems. She had many friends, for people enjoyed her companionship.

When Adah was in her early twenties she had a minor accident that gave her problems the remainder of her life. She stepped on a board hidden in tall grass; it flew up and struck her sharply on the right knee. The leg became very sore, but days passed before it was discovered that the injury had caused tuberculosis of the bone. She could no longer walk about freely and was in constant pain. At this time she was employed by a mill where seeds were graded and packaged; she was in charge of about seventy-five women.

After her father died, she and her mother moved to Montana where her brother and her sister had homesteaded. Adah and her mother decided to homestead also. She now had to use two crutches in order to move about. She secured the necessary papers from the government and her brother built a cabin twelve feet square, and even made some of the furniture. Water had to be carried to the house. Adah's right leg ached constantly and after she carried water to the house she had to rest.

Their first winter in Montana was filled with blizzards and cold winds. The lumber used in the cabin door had not been properly seasoned, and when it got wet during the first snowstorm it swelled so much it could not be closed. Heavy furniture was pushed against it, but the strong wind still blew it open. When the two women got the door shut, they nailed a carpet over it. For three days and two nights they did not go outside the cabin.

Summers were more pleasant. Adah loved the prairies covered with flowers, and wild birds came close to her as she worked in the vegetable garden.

But her health became worse. The tuberculosis spread to other parts of her body. An abcess formed in her hip bone, and she also had a hemorrhage of the lungs. At times she became despondent because it seemed she was accomplishing so little in life. She studied as much as she could, she said, "because I would dislike appearing on the other side so ignorant."

Then came the time when the doctor said she had only six months to live. Leona Hands writes of this period in Adah's life: "Sister Mae Engle Locke, women's department leader of Port Huron, learned of Adah's need and asked the Saints to fast and pray for her. The entire Eastern Michigan District set a day for fasting and prayer. Adah began to improve. During a long convalescence of more than three years, she studied earnestly. A number of quarterlies were sent to her by her niece, Stella Bailey. These, along with the Three

Standard Books, were the basis of her study. Little did she realize at the time that she was laying the foundation for years of effective teaching to come."

Following the death of her mother in 1930, Adah moved back to Port Huron and made her home with Sister Bailey. When she was asked to teach a class of sixteen junior-age boys and girls in the church school she did not realize how far-reaching her service would go. All the children's classes of the church school met in the basement. There was noise from voices and moving chairs. Adah Webb has a soft voice and it was difficult for the juniors to hear her. "I would like to conduct the class in the kitchen," she said. And her request was granted. Being by themselves gave the students a better chance to learn and to participate. They loved Adah, and she loved them. Attendance was always good because classes were always interesting.

Her students grew older and became members of the young people's class. Other juniors moved into the "kitchen class." Using her crutch to support her frail body she continued to teach junior class after junior class.

Parents were aware of the interest their children expressed in the class. Past students would say to a junior age sister or brother, "You will like Aunt Adah. I did." And often they would manage to return to visit her classes. Eventually Adah Webb became known as "Aunt" to all the children and youth of the branch.

For years Adah was Herald House book steward for Port Huron Branch. She could quickly give a review of every book published by Herald House. She also assisted with junior church and Oriole and Skylark programs.

As she grew older and weaker she made her home with Mrs. Grace Farmer in Port Huron. Poor health kept her from regular church attendance, but twice a month she taught a class of church women who went to her home for the class.

In her seventies she entered a rest home. Here she continued to read and study the Book of Mormon. Friends gave her subscriptions to church periodicals as gifts.

Her students have held positions at Herald House, Graceland College, the Independence Sanitarium and Hospital, and in the Auditorium, as well as in the business world. They have helped to carry the restored gospel throughout the States and to other countries.

"A good teacher like Adah Webb," says one of them, "doesn't merely teach a group of noisy children in the church kitchen; she teaches the whole world." Adah died May 3, 1970.

MAXINE

FRANKLIN

T oday it takes about a hundred people to do the job started in 1927 by a young woman working at the Independence Sanitarium and Hospital.

It was in 1927 that Maxine Franklin went to work as the office staff of the "San." She kept the books, paid the bills, handled the payroll, did the paper work of admitting and releasing patients, kept income tax records for employees, and made statistical and other reports. She also operated the phone and switchboard and, because she did not like to waste a minute, folded and marked linens in her free time.

Born November 10, 1901, in Harlan, Iowa, she dreamed as a child of becoming a librarian. Both her parents were studious and impressed upon her the importance of study. Her mother was the first woman in Harlan to serve on the school board and her father persuaded a wealthy man of the community to establish a public library. During her last year in high school, Maxine worked in this library. Although during her junior year she had to spend eight months in bed because of rheumatic fever, she was able to be graduated in 1920. This long illness greatly impaired her health. Never again was she able to stand for long periods of time.

She was baptized in Harlan and attended the local church with her parents, three sisters, and brother. After high school she was a student at Graceland College for two years. Here she had the honor of helping to organize the Crescent Society and was also a member of the O.O.H. Club (the first sorority of Graceland).

For a year she taught fifth grade in Denison, Iowa. Just two weeks before the close of school, she suffered another attack of rheumatic fever. Although too weak to walk she insisted on continuing her assignment as a teacher. Every day a taxi driver took her to the school building, carried her inside, came again at the end of the school day, carried her to the taxi, and took her home.

Once more she had to spend eight months in bed. The local doctor told her, "I doubt very much if you will ever walk again by yourself." She was twenty-one years old and weighed only sixty-seven pounds. But she and others prayed. She was determined to get well. Eventually she could get out of bed and sit in a chair. Then, with a person on each side of her, she was able to take steps.

One sister had married and was living in Montana. "Come visit us. The mountain air will help you." As soon as Maxine was strong enough, she went to Montana. When her health improved, she took correspondence courses in business studies. And in her sister's home she taught a kindergarten class composed of her niece and children of the neighborhood.

She returned home to Harlan much stronger. Her father had died, and her brother was attending Graceland. Maxine, her mother, and sisters decided to move to Independence, Missouri. They bought a house near Stone Church.

Some of her former Graceland classmates came to visit her and at a picnic they held in her honor it was suggested that she might get employment in Kansas City. She applied and immediately was hired in a business office. For two years she made the daily bus trip to and from Kansas City.

Then in May 1927, Gertrude Copeland, superintendent of the Independence Sanitarium and Hospital, asked her to become the "office staff." From then until 1967, when she retired, Maxine dedicated her life to service at the "San."

She saw the hospital grow in size, staff, and equipment. The few accounts that she had once kept expanded into numerous books and microfilm records and a bookkeeping machine was installed.

Besides her regular work she always had an interest in the School of Nursing and served as sponsor of several classes; in this role she helped students plan social and recreational activities during their three years of training.

About ten women who had been members of the O.O.H. Club in Graceland College were now living in Independence and often got together for friendly social meetings. They decided that as a service project they would assist out-of-town student nurses by being their "town mothers." Meetings were held once a month. Every September a tea was held in which the student nurses of the new class were introduced to their town mothers.

Maxine continued to live in the house that she and her family had purchased when they moved to Independence. Nurses came often to visit or to attend parties held for them. After Maxine had worked twenty-five years at the Sanitarium, a reception was held in her honor. Among the guests were President W. Wallace and Sister Rosamond Smith. Impressive gifts were presented to Sister Franklin.

During these years she was also active in church work. She taught a junior high class that met every Sunday in the unfinished Auditorium. Later she taught classes for primaries and beginners in Stone Church and West College congregations.

In 1956 she became interested in the Ministry to the Blind program and became a student of Braille. She was the second person in Independence to secure a certificate from the Library of Congress as a Braille transcriber. At first she wrote with a punch and perforated slate. Then she purchased a Braille writer which enabled her to work faster and do more for the church. She has transcribed Arthur Oakman's book *He Who Is*, church periodicals, tracts, part of the Book of Mormon, vacation church school studies, and textbooks for blind children.

During the forty years that she was employed at the Sanitarium she was absent only two weeks because of sickness. When she retired on January 5, 1967, a special service was held in her honor. She continues to live in Independence, but her influence grew into distant places and reaches many people. She can look with satisfaction on those whose lives she has touched during her years at the Sanitarium, the student nurses she has guided, the children and youth she has taught, the town mothers she has consulted, and the blind people for whom she has Brailled information which, without her services, they would never have had.

JESSIE

WARD

LEBARON

Many people today are members of this church because they or their parents or their grandparents read *The Call at Evening* by Jessie Ward. It is one of the most popular missionary books ever written, yet the author at one time declared, "I will never defend Joseph Smith or the Book of Mormon."

Jessie was born October 23, 1885, at Farmington, Iowa. Her parents, John and Ella Ward, were good Christian people. Her paternal grandfather, who lived with them, was an infidel and delighted in ridiculing their religious beliefs.

Because the Wards lived near Nauvoo, Illinois, they heard about Joseph Smith and his church, but no one in the Ward family made an effort to investigate the faith.

Jessie recalls the first Latter Day Saint she ever saw: "A pale, sickly little woman with a sparkle in her eye and the love of God in her heart, which she manifested outwardly toward her neighbors. The picture she made is still in my mind as she came to visit us—too weak to walk, carried like a child in the arms of her sturdy husband. How we came to love her and lean on her leadership. She did not criticize our religious understanding; never once did she suggest we were wrong. But before we knew it, she had engaged the schoolhouse and sent out her invitation, 'Come and hear my minister.' "

The missionary came, and the Wards attended. Jessie and her sisters listened attentively. At the close of the series Jessie's parents and her sisters, Nora and Hattie, asked to be baptized. Jessie hesitated. Perhaps she was thinking of remarks by her grandfather. "I'll get baptized," she told her family, "but I will never defend Joseph Smith or the Book of Mormon." On March 3, 1896, at the age of eleven, she was baptized in Lick Creek, Van Buren County, Iowa. A few days later she was at school when some of the students started ridiculing the church. Jessie defended it with fervor, proving her points as best she could. Suddenly she realized what she was doing and said to herself, "I do believe the church is true. I will defend it and everything it represents."

She attended high school at Farmington, Iowa, and was graduated in 1903. Her first employment was keeping books at a local woolen mill. Then in 1907 the Wards and several other families moved west, settling in Chehalis, Washington. Missionaries often stopped at the Ward home to eat a meal or to stay a few days. The

161

Wards and their guests spent many evenings discussing the doctrine of the church and telling about spiritual experiences they had had. Four miles north in Centralia, Washington, a branch was organized. The Wards did much to bring this branch into existence.

One Sunday morning in 1915 Jessie was working at her place of employment as a secretary. It was not her custom to work overtime, and she was unhappy about not being able to attend services. She was a good student and frequently taught classes at church school. As she worked she noticed a young engineer sitting in the manager's private office, his face buried in his hands. She thought that he might be sick. Then he came to her and, sitting on one corner of her desk, said, "I would give anything in the world if I could only believe."

"Believe what?" she asked. He said that he wished he could believe there was a God. He was concerned about whether the story of creation as given in the Bible was true. She tried to explain her belief to him. That evening she very carefully studied the first chapters of Genesis and other books available. She put her studies into writing, thinking she would show it to the young engineer and also read it at the church program called Religio. Unfortunately the young man was killed before she had a chance to show him her notes. Since his remarks impressed her so greatly she felt that others must be asking the same questions.

For the next two years she did more writing. Chapter by chapter, she was writing *The Call at Evening* but she did not realize it. After she had completed seven chapters, she began to lose interest and wondered if it was worth spending more of her time on it. She sent the seven chapters to Elbert A. Smith, editor of *Autumn Leaves,* and asked his advice. On the corner of the front page she wrote, "Is this worth finishing?"

Time went by, and she did not hear from him. She thought that he was too busy to read the manuscript. Then it came back, but to her surprise it was not the rough copy she had sent him. It was neatly retyped, and with it was a letter saying, "Finish as rapidly as possible."

Encouraged, she went to work again. When Brother Elbert became quite sick, she stopped writing. Then came a letter from Sister Smith saying Elbert wanted to know how soon he could have the manuscript to publish in serial form in *Autumn Leaves.* Again she began working on the book.

She found that more than the ability to write was needed; spiritual guidance was essential. She knew people would read the book and trust it. Over and over she prayed, "Lord, somebody will form an opinion from what I write, and I don't know enough to write it." In the process of writing she was blessed with outstanding vision and guidance.

In 1918 *The Call at Evening* was continued in serial form in *Autumn Leaves.* The first chapters were published before the book was completed. Jessie, working to support herself, could spend only evenings writing. Eventually the story was complete, and in 1920 it was published in book form. Few copies of the early printing are still available. These sold immediately, and a second edition was printed. That also sold immediately. In all, it went to press twenty-eight times. The record of how many copies were printed has been lost, but the estimate is 100,000.

A sister, Melva Crum, has prepared this biographical information about Jessie:

"She served as clerk for the city of Centralia, Washington, for many years and during that time wrote several pageants for church, and Easter and Christmas programs. One major work, 'And It Came to Pass,' was presented by the churches of Centralia involving the combined choirs of the city plus the music department of the high school. It started with the Annunciation and ended with the Resurrection. It was a thrilling thing to see the city clergymen as the twelve apostles portraying the laying on of hands for healing the sick, especially when some of them did not practice this. The chief of police played the part of Pilate very touchingly. A local woman of the streets who had been converted came to Jessie and begged to be allowed to play Mary Magdalene. This two-hour pageant was so dramatic and moving that the huge audience sat down when the final 'Hallelujah Chorus' was ended, not wanting to break the spell.

"Jessie also wrote several pageants for Centralia's Pioneer Days celebrations and on one occasion asked if the reservation Indians in the area would like to participate. They were delighted and offered to set up an Indian tepee village in the arena at the fair grounds where the pageant was to be held. When she asked them if they would stage an Indian war dance, she discovered they had no such ritual, so she went to the reservation, taught them tom-tom rhythms, and then set out to teach sixty braves how to do a war dance. She would

164

laugh heartily at the picture she must have made—a lone white woman surrounded by serious Indian men trying to learn a war dance."

In later life Jessie was married to Dr. Glenn LeBaron. They made their home in Seattle, Washington, where Jessie took courses at the university. After Dr. Le-Baron's death in 1953, Jessie continued to live in their Seattle home.

In April 1967, the women of the Seattle District held a banquet in her honor. Apostle Donald V. Lents was the guest speaker. Barbara Cothern, women's leader of the district, was in charge of the banquet. Then on December 12, 1968, Jessie went to live at Resthaven in Independence, Missouri. Her book is still in the libraries of many homes and churches and continues to serve as a missionary aid.

She died September 1, 1970, at Resthaven. She is buried in Mound Grove Cemetery, Independence, Missouri.

GLADYS

GOULD

Gladys sat quietly beside her father as he drove the creaking wagon across the field road of the Gould farm. Looking out across the land she wondered what it had been like years before when the Chippewa and Sioux tribes had fought each other near Battle Lake, which was visible in the distance.

Her father slipped his firm arm about her and said, "Gladys, you are now eight years old. Have you thought about being baptized when we attend reunion this summer?" As they rode they talked about the importance of this ordinance, and Gladys made her decision to be baptized.

She was born on February 6, 1895, on the family

166

homestead ten miles east. When she was seven they had moved to this farm near Battle Lake because it was nearer to a church congregation at Clitherall, Minnesota. She was the youngest of a family of six girls and two boys. Homelife was happy and interesting. During winter evenings when the temperature sometimes sank to fifty below zero, the family enjoyed games, singing around the organ, or reading beside the big heating stove.

Gladys was baptized June 25, 1903, at Clitherall Reunion. It was then that she decided to serve the church the rest of her life. She admired three of her older sisters who were schoolteachers. She liked to "dress up" in their skirts and pretend to be teaching school. She would go into the attic where the pumpkins and squashes were stored during the winter, place them in rows, and pretend they were her pupils.

One of the things she enjoyed most in childhood was visiting the home of her grandparents, Lewis and Jannette Whiting. They had been children in Nauvoo at the time Joseph Smith had been killed and had many interesting stories to tell. Gladys also enjoyed reading. Always she was trying to learn more. When she was fifteen she decided to read the Book of Mormon carefully and thoughtfully. It took her a month. When she read the promise in Moroni 10:4, 5, she sensed so deeply the love of God that she began to cry. Embarrassed, she went away to a place alone, rereading the words and asking herself, "Why should I feel like this?" The answer given her was, "This is the power by which men shall know that the book is true." Then she knelt and thanked God for this unsought testimony which became a strength to her many times in the future.

When she was seventeen she passed the examinations and received a certificate to teach. Her first school was located about fifty miles from her home. She spent summers thereafter taking courses at the State Normal School at Moorhead, Minnesota, or at the teachers' institutes at the county seat.

She wrote to a friend: "My first school was in a Scandinavian district, and I learned to say the Lord's Prayer in Norwegian, to eat flatbread, lefse, and ludefisk, but I would not drink their coffee. Another term was spent among the Germans who fed me pickled fish, blood sausage and pudding, and wild ducks. In a Finnish community I learned to take the Finnish steam baths in a specially prepared bathhouse with its large fireplace and steaming boiler. In this school of forty pupils I struggled with ten beginners who could not speak or understand English. Among all these nationalities, I found kindhearted people, interesting to know. The last of my seven years of teaching was in my own home district where my mother had taught in pioneer days."

When her parents moved to Independence, Missouri, Gladys moved with them. She enrolled at Graceland College and took a secretarial course.

In October 1921, she was hired as the first secretary to work for the Auditorium, which was then in the planning stages. She was employed by the church architect, Henry C. Smith, whose office was near the Stone Church. Later the office was moved to the Battery Block where other church offices were located.

Because church officials did not have enough secretaries to handle the increasing work, they often asked Gladys for assistance. That first year she took dictation from sixty people; among these were E. L. Kelley, F. A. Smith, R. S. Salyards, C. B. Hartshorn, B. R. McGuire, R. V. Hopkins, M. A. and Ida Etzenhouser, and J. A. Becker. When missionaries were in Independence for a few days, they also came to her office to dictate letters.

She saw the Auditorium basement dug by men and teams of horses. She saw the massive framework of the building put into place. She heard dubious people say, "There will never be enough church members to fill it . . . it's a waste of money."

By 1928 the building was completed enough to have some offices moved into it; among the first was the one in which she worked. Other secretaries were hired. Offices were crowded, and there was always the noise of construction.

In November 1942 she was transferred from the office of the Presiding Bishopric to the office of the First Presidency. Her first assignment was to take dictation from President Frederick M. Smith for two and a half hours. She took her shorthand notebook home that evening and did the transcribing. After the death of "Frederick M." Israel A. Smith became the president of the church, and Gladys continued to work in the office of the First Presidency. Israel would take home the letters he had received, jot out answers in longhand, and bring these in to her early the next morning. W. Wallace Smith, who became the next president, shared her interest in gardening. Frequently they would bring flowers to the office.

Gladys worked in the Auditorium during the trying days of the depression when many people could not give money to the church because they were unemployed. She saw the dedication of Bishop G. Leslie DeLapp as he struggled to pay off the debt on the Auditorium. She read letters written by Saints in many parts of the world who sacrificed to pay this debt and keep the building for the church.

At one time Presiding Patriarch Elbert A. Smith came to the office of the First Presidency every morning to collect his mail. Often he would bring dictaphone cylinders of letters and blessings to Gladys for transcription.

Doing secretarial work for the church architect, four presiding bishops, two presiding evangelists, and three prophets over a period of thirty-eight years gave Gladys ample opportunity for church service, but she served in other ways than as a secretary in the Auditorium. A gifted writer, she has contributed to all the periodicals of the church. She has taught in church school and vacation church school and served as secretary of the Gudgell Park congregation. She has been a Skylark leader, taught Light of Life classes for seven years, and served as chairman of the Light of Life program in Center Stake. She urged girls to take advantage of the training and inspiration offered by the Light of Life program: "Your assurance will grow that Jesus Christ, the Son of God, is the light of this world, the light that can glorify your own life and bring its greatest joys."

Gladys retired from her job at the Auditorium in 1960. This has given her time to write, garden, and travel. In 1966 she wrote from Clitherall, Minnesota, where she was vacationing: "I have cut a road through the forest, dug up sod, planted a vegetable garden, trimmed out young trees between my cabin and the lake, and walked three miles a day to the mailbox." Such "recreation" is well deserved, for the years she spent as a church secretary were truly years of dedicated labor.

ALICE

BURGESS

Although she was eight years old when she was baptized, she had already been serving three years as a missionary for the church. Alice M. Chase, daughter of Amos M. and Eliza France Chase, was born October 15, 1892, in Lamoni, Iowa, and baptized there on March 30, 1900. Her father was a professional photographer and her mother helped with the "retouching."

When Alice was four and her brother Charles seven, their father left on a mission for the church to the Pacific Northwest. A few months later, Sister Chase and the two children made the smoky, cindery four-day trip by train to join Elder Chase. During the summer, the church furnished a large "gospel tent" in which church services were conducted and two smaller tents for living quarters. Each meeting was preceded by a song service. It was here that Alice learned to enjoy singing. Later, the four members of the family sang together and were known as the Chase Quartet. Besides assisting with the singing, Alice and Charles helped to distribute tracts and announcements, knocking on every door in town.

During the winter months, Sister Chase and the children lived in a cottage. She found work with the local photographer, and the money she earned helped support them. In those early years she often sent back to the church some of the small family allowance received each month. She also made clothes for Alice. Brother Chase often told his daughter, "Remember that one who is with God is always one who is in the majority." So she held her head high when she was wearing cardboard-patched shoes and felt she was fortunate to be serving the church of Jesus Christ.

During the years she was growing to womanhood, she moved often with her parents while her father served as a missionary. "About every two years," she says, "I attended a different school because Father's assignments took him to various places." She started school in Seattle, Washington, and spent seven years at various times in Utah. Occasionally the family returned to live a year or so at their home in Lamoni. It was in one of these periods that Alice was baptized. "To grow up in Lamoni," she recalls, "was a rich experience."

Alice enjoyed hearing her grandmother, Sarah Chase, talk about her experiences in Nauvoo. She told how she went from Maine to Nauvoo in 1842, walking almost all the way. She shared memories of singing in the Temple Choir in the Grove in Nauvoo, and of hearing Joseph

Smith, Jr., preach. She was present when Joseph Smith III was brought forth and set aside to succeed his father.

Because Elder Chase's health began to fail, the family moved for two years to a farm in Oklahoma. Alice enjoyed farm life and especially delighted in riding horses. She took her last two years of high school in Alva, Oklahoma.

Again her father served as a missionary in the state of Utah, and again Alice assisted with the music. In a letter published in a church paper, Elder Chase wrote, "We are preaching on the streets. The family will assist. We want to do what we can to do the greatest good to the greatest number of our district." That remark seemed to become the motto for Alice, for she always tried to "do the greatest good to the greatest number of people."

These street services were dignified and orderly, and there were often several hundred people waiting each night as the Chase family arrived at the appointed corner. One summer Alice and her brother organized an orchestra of young people. While in Utah Alice attended the University of Utah for three years, majoring in Latin and minoring in German and English. She was elected a member of the English Honor Society there.

Alice had great admiration for her mother. Wherever her father was doing missionary work, her mother visited homes. Sister Chase organized local women to help in homes where there was sickness. She was a good student and completed many study courses. "The women under her stimulus," wrote Alice years later, "were always studying." Both Brother and Sister Chase completed extension courses from Graceland.

Alice attended Cornell University in Ithaca, New

174

York, and received a B.A. degree in Latin and German. She also became a member of the Cornell Dramatic Club. She was graduated in 1914. In Ithaca there was no RLDS Church, so she sang in the Baptist choir and taught a young people's class in a Methodist church. Both groups knew about her church and respected her for respecting it.

When the time came for Alice to begin her career as a teacher, she wrote to Graceland College and applied for a position on the staff. S. A. Burgess, president of the college, informed her that there were no openings. She then obtained a position teaching Latin and German at Lamoni High School.

She had been teaching only a few weeks when the high school building burned, and classes had to be held at the college. Here Alice became better acquainted with President Burgess. A lawyer, he had given up a promising practice in St. Louis, Missouri, to serve the church. Romance developed, and they were married in Lamoni on June 15, 1915. Some of the pupils jokingly accused her of burning down the school for the purpose of meeting Sam Burgess.

In the fall of 1915 Brother Burgess was appointed Fellow at Clark University. Although he had an A.B. and M. A. in law, President F. M. Smith encouraged him to go, so he and Alice moved to Worcester, Massachusetts. While her husband was attending the university, Alice also continued her education. She took additional vocal lessons and in 1916 she received a Master's degree in education and psychology at Clark.

In 1917, before he had completed his thesis and formal exams for his Ph.D., Brother Burgess was asked to return to Lamoni and take charge of Herald House. This he did. For one year (1917-18) Alice taught German, English, and psychology at Graceland. While the Burgesses were still living in Lamoni two daughters were born to them, Eveline and Florence.

When Herald House was moved to Independence, the Burgess family moved also. It was about this time that Brother Burgess became completely deaf following mastoid surgery.

Ruth Lyman Smith asked Alice to assist with the church's program for girls. She edited a column for young women in the church publication called *Autumn Leaves* and became very active in the Oriole program.

In 1920 an organization called Temple Builders was started for the young women. By a World Conference vote the Department of Women was asked to prepare a "course of mothercraft for the girls of the church until such time as the public schools shall include such instruction in their curriculums." Alice Burgess organized this program. The manual of the Temple Builders was printed in Lamoni in June 1920. A girl had to be fifteen years old to become a member. The uniform was the middy-blouse dress popular at the time.

In 1926 a pageant, "The Miracle," came to Kansas City. Players traveled with the pageant, but a ten-part chorus of forty voices was needed to accompany the drama. One thousand five hundred local people tried out for this chorus. Among the forty chosen was Alice Burgess. "I never dreamed I would be selected," she told her husband. "I can't possibly go over there every night for weeks to rehearse." "Alice," said her husband, "This is an opportunity you must not pass up. I will see that

the house and the girls are taken care of. You sing in
'The Miracle' and you learn all you can about producing
a pageant." Alice accepted the challenge and did learn
much. A few years later she put the knowledge to use
for the church.

One of the outstanding accomplishments of Alice
Burgess took place in 1930 when the World Church was
celebrating the centennial of the restoration of the
gospel. At the request of the First Presidency, Brother
and Sister Burgess wrote a pageant that was presented in
the partly completed Auditorium. Hundreds of people
were in the cast. It was called "Fulfillment—a Pageant of
the Restoration" and covered three epochs—Christ's
message, the Reformation, and the Restoration. A
reporter wrote about her, "She was asked to do in a few
months what ordinarily would have required a year or
more. She has written a pageant which will bring a thrill
of religious emotion and stir the loyalty and purpose of
every Christian, and particularly every Latter Day
Saint."

Alice also wrote a twenty-six-part radio drama, "A
Modern Prophet," on the life of Joseph Smith, Jr. This
brought the story of the restored gospel to hundreds of
people who otherwise would never have heard it. The
broadcast was particularly effective since it was presented during the "prime time" vesper hour on Sundays.

She has written ten quarterlies that have been used in
the church school. Many of these were written at the
request of Brother C. B. Woodstock and included such
subjects as "The Call of the Church," "The Call to
Christian Personality," "Gospel Principles of the Restoration," "Religion and Culture in the Home," and

"The Latter Day Saint Home for Today and Tomorrow."

Among her other written works are study courses for the Department of Women. In collaboration with her daughter, Eveline, she prepared two lengthy dramas, "The Elect Lady" and "Henceforth, Friends." She and her husband wrote two other Conference pageants in addition to "Fulfillment. . . ." One of them, "Revelation," was given at the Conference held in a large tent on the Campus grounds before the Auditorium was even partially completed.

Like Ruth Lyman Smith, Alice Burgess thought it important that women understand the laws of their lands and vote. Some women felt that they should not have the bother of voting. At one time when Alice gave a talk stressing the importance of women voting and being concerned with civic affairs her audience stood up and walked out. Before many years these same women learned that her remarks were wise and that the church approved of her teaching.

For years she was a radio singer. She sang contralto solos in the *Messiah* and *Elijah* and in Music Club productions. In drama she was active with the White Masque Players. She also sang in quartets and the Stone Church Choir.

Then she had a "conversion experience" directing her toward the Women's Department. President F. M. Smith asked her to become leader of the Center Stake Women. Part of her experience in this call was to organize the Young Matrons.

On November 24, 1950, Brother Burgess died. He had served as president of Graceland College, editor of the

178

Saints' Herald, World Church Historian, and research assistant to the First Presidency.

In 1954 Alice was asked by the First Presidency to serve as the director of the General Department of Women. Of this she wrote, "Perhaps the greatest personal blessing came to me through my almost constant contact and fellowship with the women of the church—personal fellowship in institutes, retreats, workshops, reunions, and General Conference classes." Under her leadership the department expanded and new ideas and methods were implemented. She served in this office until 1958.

After retirement she taught women's classes—as many as forty a year in various congregations. Today she lives in Independence and continues to study and to serve the church.

ALICE
EDWARDS

The first thing Alice Myrmida Smith saw when she was lifted from the water of the baptismal font was the white whiskers of her grandfather, Joseph Smith III. Alice loved this man. To other people he was the president of the church, but to her he was a grandfather with a gentle voice and a pleasant laugh.

Alice was born March 29, 1899, in Lamoni, Iowa. When she was only a few years old two important things happened in her life. Her father, Frederick M. Smith, was ordained a counselor to her grandfather; this made him a member of the First Presidency of the church. Being only a few years old, Alice understood little of the meaning of this at the time. The second thing she discovered was that there was a different world beyond

180

her immediate environment. With her mother she made a trip to California to visit an aunt. Here she saw for the first time the sandy beach at the edge of the ocean. Because the only sand she had seen was in her sandbox in the backyard, she was awed by so much sand—and so much water.

With her parents, she moved in 1906 to Independence, Missouri. Alice enjoyed exploring the new house and was always following her father as he worked about it. When plans were being made for building it, her father had said, "There are three things I want in this house—wide doorways, a large bathtub, and lots of bookcases." Alice knew he wanted the wide doors and the big bathtub because he was a large man. And she knew he wanted bookcases because he was a student and delighted in studying. Her father did the plumbing in the house and also installed both the electricity and gas. Alice, watching him, realized the joy of learning to master such skills.

The same year that Alice was baptized—1907—her sister Lois was born. Because her mother was not well it was necessary for Alice to help with the housework and care of her sister. On numerous occasions after President Smith returned from his day at the office and Alice from school they would do the family laundry. He would turn the wringer on the washing machine while she put the clothes through it. Then because he was mechanically inclined, he constructed a means of operating the wringer by electricity.

In 1908 and 1909 her father attended the University of Kansas. When he received his Master's degree, he took the diploma to the home of his father and, laying the roll in the hand of his blind father said, "This is my Master's degree." Joseph Smith III, who had wanted an academic education, constantly encouraged his sons and daughters to work toward higher education.

Because her father's work caused the family to move frequently, Alice attended high school in four different places—Independence, Lamoni, Worcester, and Kansas City.

When she attended school in Lamoni she lived for a while in the home of her uncle and aunt, Mr. and Mrs. P. A. Silsby. Alice had the misfortune to break her leg while playing on the girls' basketball team. The physician who took care of her, Dr. Bertha Greer, was a member of the church. During the time that Alice's leg was in a cast, Dr. Greer came to her home every morning and drove her to school. It was also during this year that Alice helped Mrs. S. A. Burgess with the first Oriole handbook.

When her father decided to obtain his Ph.D. from Clark University, the family moved in 1914 to Worcester, Massachusetts, where Lois attended grade school and Alice high school.

Recalling the days in Worcester, Alice relates, "Lois was always bringing home stray cats. One time one of Father's big feet came down on a kitten's tail. Father was grieved. He gave the kitten first aid and put a bandage on the tail. The kitten shook it off. Father put another bandage on, and then carried the kitten around on a pillow. He kept the tail between two of his big fingers until the kitten felt better."

The busy family often received letters from Independence. Because President Smith was blind, the letters were written by Ada, his wife. Then came the sad news. Alice's grandfather was sick and not expected to live. Her mother and father returned to Missouri, but Alice and Lois remained in Worcester to attend school. Joseph Smith died December 10, 1914. After his funeral, Brother and Sister Smith returned to Massachusetts for a few months. Then in September of 1915 they moved back to their house in Independence. On October 20—less than a year after the death of Joseph—Ada also died.

Alice received special honor for her creative writing while attending the Polytechnic Institute in Kansas City, Missouri. Editors of three local newspapers were judges of a story-writing contest in which she won first place.

Cars were something new at this time. Alice learned to drive and take care of the Smith family car. "I could practically take it apart and put it together again," she says. Because her mother did not like to drive, Alice chauffeured her to many classes, meetings, and speaking engagements.

When Mrs. George H. (Cordie) Hulmes organized a number of singers to present Handel's *Messiah* for Christmas in 1916, Alice was among them. For a number of years she sang annually in this choir; she was also a member of the Stone Church Choir.

In 1920 her father and Apostle T. W. Williams toured Europe to determine the growth and needs of the church and to meet the Saints in various countries. Ruth Smith and her daughters went to California to live because she felt better in a warmer climate. In his letters home, Brother Smith wrote that a young man in England, Frank Henry Edwards, was serving as his secretary and assistant. He said the youth planned to attend Graceland College.

The *Saints' Herald* of April 19, 1922, contains the following news item: "Miss Alice Smith has been admitted to Stanford University in California. This is considered quite an honor since the number of girls is strictly limited to 500 and they have a waiting list of 1500. Selections are not made entirely on the order of application but more on the quality of recommendation." While Alice was attending the University of Southern California, F. Henry Edwards was a student at Graceland. He was ordained an apostle on October 13, 1922.

When she became acquainted with him, she agreed with her father's praise of him. In June 1923 they became engaged. She was graduated from Stanford with a B.A. degree, but she was not at the graduation service. Instead she was being married. The wedding took place in Stone Church on June 27, 1924, with her father officiating.

In 1925 she accepted the assignment to write the column "Who's Who Among Our Young People" in the church periodical, *Autumn Leaves.* She wrote of herself, "When I came home from college, the institute needed another teacher, and I taught some classes in college— English, journalism, and short-story writing. This year I am continuing these classes in my home, but I am trying to make them more advanced and more applicable to individual needs than the organized classes could possibly be. In all this I have in mind especially training writers for our church papers and have the pleasure of

seeing some of my proteges' material already in print."
Thus began a work that was to grow and expand—the
training of writers to serve the church. Alice and Frank
Edwards had four children—Lyman, David, Ruth, and
Paul. Lyman and David were twins but David died in
infancy. Alice enjoyed her children and delighted in
watching them master skills. In one of her writings she
says, "I have always felt that summer vacation is an
opportunity to get acquainted with my own children,
although it seems strenuous with my backyard full of
my own and my neighbors' children. I realize that it is
also a precious experience. It is something that once
past can be reclaimed only in memory."

Indeed, the backyard of the Edwards home was the
gathering place for children of the community. One
time she noticed a police car going by the house
frequently and police watching the noisy children at
play. When the police parked nearby, she asked if
something was wrong. "Lady," explained the police-
man, "we have reports that some child is stealing from
garages. We thought he might be back there in your
yard, but we know he is not. All those children are too
dirty and too happy to think about stealing."

Like her parents she was interested in helping
children whose troubled lives had brought them under
the jurisdiction of the civic courts. She worked with the
courts, helping a number of young people, and even
took three children into her home and made them part
of the household.

Following the death of her mother on May 4, 1926,
her father was lonely. He depended on his daughters,

Alice and Lois (now Mrs. Edward Larson), to assist him with social functions.

From 1938 to 1945 Alice was a member of the General Council of Women. She wrote articles for church publications, made talks, and taught classes, all in the interest of the women of the church.

Her father died March 20, 1946. Israel A. Smith, who became the next president of the church, selected her husband as a counselor. Brother Edwards frequently traveled to other countries for the church. In one of his books, *The Whole Wide World,* he says, "When I left home this time, we talked about the gifts to bring home to the children. My wife said to me, 'Bring yourself back to us; bring back the message that you take away with you.' "

Author of a number of church books, Brother Edwards in talking about them once said, "My wife is my severest and best critic. She reads and checks my manuscripts. My writings always improve under the actions of her blue pencil."

When Israel Smith died and his younger brother, W. Wallace Smith, became the president of the church, Brother Edwards continued as a counselor.

Alice was on the committee that prepared *The Hymnal* which was first printed by the church in 1956. In the foreword it is said of Alice: "Her specialty lies in the field of literature, particularly poetic literature; and this special training was frequently utilized by the committee." She had also done editorial work on an earlier hymnal which was published by the church in 1933.

A number of her poems were compiled in a private

edition called *Personally Yours*. A copy of this book was donated to the Pauline Arnson Memorial Library in the headquarters office of the Department of Women.

Using only scriptures, she arranged the words for the cantata "The Song of the Restoration" which was first presented at the World Conference of 1960. This impressive cantata, with music composed by Warren Martin, has been reproduced on tape recordings.

Interested in community work, she was one of the women responsible for starting the Independence unit of the League of Women Voters and served as the vice-president. She was also one of the founders of the Tuesday Club.

When her children were grown, she was asked by Blanche Green to teach English to a group of soldiers who had just come home from the war and who needed this training to return to employment or school. Although in poor health at the time, she agreed to teach the class. When it was completed, the men asked her to teach subjects that would give them credits which they could apply at college. The University of Kansas permitted her to teach an extension class in English. During the next few years she taught additional classes in English and creative writing.

Then she herself returned to school to further her education: "My return to school in the late '40's represents the stripe people tend to draw down the center of their lives and call middle age. Before this my concerns were with my family, my personal friends, my church, an occasional PTA lecture, and similar matters. After this a whole new world opened to me."

She taught and attended classes at the University of

Kansas City (later the University of Missouri at Kansas City), and in 1954 received her Master's degree. Having completed this, she taught at KCU and began working toward a doctorate at the University of Kansas. She passed the qualifying examination and completed half of her thesis when again her health began to fail. She found it necessary to do less teaching.

Besides her university classes in English and creative writing, she taught English, children's literature, and introduction to literature at the Jackson County Center of the Central Missouri State College. She also taught English and creative writing at the School of the Restoration. For several years she taught English at the "San" School of Nursing.

She served several years on the executive committee of the RLDS Professional Teachers Association. She is a member of the Association of American Women of the University Club and helped conduct a book reviewing group for it. At one time she served as assistant editor of the *Piano Tuners' Journal,* and for several years wrote advertising for *Cox Features.*

For two years the Edwards served as leaders of the "Great Books" group in Independence and were instrumental in bringing an understanding of great books of literature to interested people.

Alice has done a considerable amount of lecturing and public speaking. She has spoken often at PTA meetings (she has been an active PTA member). She has also lectured for women of the church and for groups of people interested in journalism and creative writing.

To a class of writers, she stated, "God certainly sends us the initial impulse to write, and sometimes the actual

188

words with which to begin our task, but he has also endowed us with the ability to examine, rethink, and revise the work which we do. My own experience has been that innumerable revisions and a great many hours are essential to an even passable piece of work."

She has devoted countless hours to training people to serve the church through their creative writing talent. She affirms, "Some people, by putting their minds to it, can produce work, and good work, on a given subject or in a given area." When the Creative Writers' Guild was organized she assisted by teaching classes and lecturing. Writers could always depend on her to take an interest in their honest attempts to serve the church. And in addition to helping many people with their writing she has always been available to help people with their personal living problems.

The three children of Brother and Sister Edwards are now married and in homes of their own. There are eight grandchildren. The Edwards are retired and live in Independence. She says, "I am not interested in making a record of how many people I have helped to do creative writing, but I am interested in those people making good records of service with the knowledge I have shared."

MARGARET

GIBSON

"This is about the most wonderful thing that has ever happened to me," Margaret Wilson said to herself as she accepted the certificate giving her a scholarship to Syracuse University. It was 1913, and she was being graduated from the high school at Mount Vernon, New York, where she lived with her family.

She was born December 17, 1895, in Springfield, Massachusetts, the daughter of Charles G. and Anna May Wilson. She had a brother, Edgar, two years younger. Her parents were members of a Protestant church. In fact, her father and grandfather had served as organists in the church.

When she was about five years old the family moved to Roxbury, Massachusetts, where she started to school. When she was nine, they moved to Mount Vernon, New York. Here she continued grade school and attended high school.

The Wilsons had a home filled with happiness and love, but there were times of financial difficulty. There was a depression when they lived in Mount Vernon and her father was out of work and the family existed on the small wages of her brother. When Christmas came that year they hoped to have some inexpensive meat for their dinner, but Margaret's grandmother used part of her savings to purchase a turkey. It was small, but it represented the sacrificing love that Margaret was learning.

The scholarship helped finance her college. In addition to it, she worked all the time she was attending, and her parents helped as much as possible. In 1917 she was graduated with a B.A. degree in English and a minor in German.

Something else of great importance happened at college. She met Archie L. Gibson. Both were members of the same Protestant church. At the beginning of World War II he enlisted. While he was away they wrote letters, making plans for their future. After the war he returned home and completed his college education.

During his absence Margaret taught in the high school in Richfield Spring, New York, and the Vocational High School in Newton, Massachusetts. They were married on July 15, 1920, in her parents' home, then went to Harrogate, Tennessee, where Archie taught in Lincoln Memorial University. The following year he secured civil service employment as a forest ranger in a park in Wyoming. Part of his work was to mark trees that could be cut down by the Standard Lumber Company. In order to be with her husband, Margaret moved to Wyoming and lived in the park. During this time, she did a lot of reading and studying. "I felt that I wanted a greater challenge in life and religion than I had had up to this time," she said. She taught in a small local school, and she and Archie held church school in their home for children of the people who worked for the lumber company.

Later her husband was transferred to the Wyoming National Forest at Afton where he served as an entomologist working to control insect destruction of the trees. It was here that Margaret Gibson experienced a great joy, a deep sorrow, and began the discovery that was to illuminate the lives of both her and her husband. She did not want to move to Afton because most of the people living there were members of the Church of Jesus Christ of Latter-day Saints, and she had heard frightening things about that denomination.

A few weeks after they were settled in their new home, a son was born to them. The child was not well. Realizing that he might die, Margaret and Archie wanted him baptized—in accordance with the belief in their church. The only minister available was a member of the Church of Jesus Christ of Latter-day Saints. He refused to baptize the infant, declaring that it was not according to his belief, but he was considerate of the grieving parents, as were their neighbors who were members of the same church.

An elder of the Utah church gave the Gibsons his

personal copy of the Book of Mormon to read. Years later Margaret wrote about this experience: "After I started to read the Book of Mormon I found it difficult to stop, and I read for hours at a time. It was truth, and as I read I found sound and solid answers to many questions which had concerned me in the past and to which I had found no clear-cut answers in the Bible. There was nothing contrary to the Bible teachings, but the Book of Mormon made these teachings clearer. I had the testimony of the Spirit of God that the words of the ancient writers of the book were true."

However, her studies revealed to her that the Book of Mormon did not condone polygamy while the Utah edition of the Doctrine and Covenants did. She could not believe that God would ask his people to practice polygamy and at the same time say that it was evil.

Because there were no Protestant churches in the community, Margaret and Archie Gibson attended the Church of Jesus Christ of Latter-day Saints. "We enjoyed and will always be grateful for the kindness of those good people."

Parents of a small boy who was having difficulty learning to read asked Margaret Gibson to tutor him. She did, and the child became a capable reader. This experience was the beginning of a field of service in which she was to tutor other students.

Another son was born. Archie Gibson's work now took them to Coeur d'Alene where he worked in the office of the United States Forest Service. A daughter was born to them in Coeur d'Alene. Here, also, they found a church of their faith. Margaret was happy to be among people of her denomination, but she found she could no longer believe their doctrine. She could not forget the truths she had discovered in the Book of Mormon.

"I prayed very earnestly for direction," she wrote, "asking that if God had a church on earth like the New Testament church in organization, teaching, and spiritual gifts, and believing in the Book of Mormon, he would reveal it to me. I wanted to keep all the truth I had, and to receive that which I knew was also truth but which I had not yet found."

While reading a local newspaper in April 1930, Margaret saw a picture of the Auditorium in Independence, Missouri. An accompanying article told that the Reorganized Church of Jesus Christ of Latter Day Saints was erecting the building for its headquarters offices. The article also said that Dr. Frederick M. Smith, grandson of Joseph Smith, Jr., was the president of the church, and that the church believed in the Book of Mormon but did not believe in polygamy.

Margaret Gibson sensed that perhaps God was answering her prayer. She felt she must investigate this church which she had never before heard of. A few days later she saw an item about a social gathering being held at a local RLDS congregation. The name of the pastor was Elder Lawrence Holmes. She laid the newspaper down in surprise. She had visited with this man only a few days before. He was laying a hardwood floor in the home of a neighbor and she had gone to see it. She phoned Elder Holmes.

Shortly after this both Brother and Sister Holmes came to visit the Gibsons, bringing books and tracts that explained the church. They and Evangelist A. C. Martin

194

answered the questions Margaret asked. Archie agreed to her being baptized into this church but felt that he did not want to be. She was baptized November 16, 1930, by Elder Holmes.

When she spoke to her Protestant minister about this, he said that if she felt she should join the Reorganized Church then she should do it. This minister and the Gibsons remained constant friends. For several years Archie would go to his church and Margaret would go to hers. Occasionally Archie would go to church with Margaret and assist with the orchestra. They realized that attending separate churches did not contribute to a happy marriage. Twelve years later Archie joined the Reorganized Church—not because his wife was a member but because he realized that it was the church of Jesus Christ. Before they moved from Coeur d'Alene, he served several years as pastor of the congregation.

Margaret took correspondence courses from the Department of Religious Education and later other study courses. For this she received a certificate of merit because of her studies. The family attended church and frequently went to reunions at Silver Lake, Washington. Servicemen, stationed at a nearby naval base, were frequent guests in the Gibson home.

In 1947 their son was married, and in 1950 their daughter was married.

A big accomplishment in the life of Margaret Gibson was the writing of the book *Emma Smith, the Elect Lady* which was published by the church in 1954. Margaret and Archie had visited Nauvoo, Illinois, and had sat in the room where the bodies of Joseph Smith and Hyrum Smith were placed before burial. She imagined the emotions the widow Emma Smith must have had and then she thought of the continuing courage of this woman. "I should write about Emma Smith," she told herself. "There are fine women who are members of the Utah church who do not understand her." She spent many hours researching and creating the book. Copies of it are now in many private and public libraries.

The year after the book was published Archie's work for the government took them to Missoula, Montana. She enrolled at Montana State University and earned a Master's degree in education. She wrote her thesis on the problems faced by children learning to read. Since tutoring the small boy in Wyoming she had assisted many children and adults by giving private remedial reading lessons.

A principal was needed for Opportunity School in Missoula—a school for mentally and physically handicapped children. Dr. Jack Munro, an instructor at the university, suggested Margaret. For three years she served as the principal.

When asked about her experiences in this school she said, "They were delightful, loving children who had love and empathy for one another. They were good children and they had intense loyalty to their school." One girl was blind. Sister Thelona Stevens, who was in charge of the general church program of Ministry to the Blind, sent special material written in Braille for this girl. Women's organizations in Montana assisted the school by earning money for it and by working with the students.

In Missoula, Archie again served as pastor for several years.

After his retirement in June 1957, they moved to Missouri. In 1962 they settled in Blue Springs, not far from Independence. Both are busy teaching at reunions, camps, and in the Blue Springs congregation. Both work in the Zion's Hope Montessori School for young children in Independence. Margaret also assists with the Center Stake program for exceptional children.

Apostle Reed Holmes, son of Elder Lawrence Holmes, wrote: "Among those who lent encouragement in my youth was Margaret Gibson. When algebra and geometry threatened to throw me she tutored. When laziness prompted satisfaction with mediocrity, she prodded. And when I left home to find some niche to fill, she handed me a note to read in times of discouragement. I'm grateful for a good teacher and friend."

RUTH

HOLMAN

When Ruth Lewis was primary age she did something that few girls have a chance to do—she started school twice, and each time on a different side of the world. When she was six years old, she started to school in St. Joseph, Missouri. When she was seven, she entered school in Cardiff, Wales. "That was the beginning of my being able to attend schools in many different places of the world. I was lucky in having a father who was a missionary for the church," she wrote when she was grown.

Her parents had been born in Wales and had migrated to the United States as children with their parents. Both had become members of the Reorganized Church in Ohio in 1866. Ruth was born June 23, 1894, in St.

Joseph, Missouri, the youngest of nine children.

For many years her father, William Lewis, owned and operated a wholesale and retail creamery. He also served as the pastor of the congregation in St. Joseph and as president of Far West District, but he wanted to return to Wales to preach the gospel.

Shortly after Ruth had started to school, President Joseph Smith III and Bishop E. L. Kelley made a surprise visit to the Lewis home. While her father visited with the men, Ruth helped her mother, Mary Lewis, get the evening meal. Then she heard why the men had come to visit; they wanted her father to return to Wales as a missionary. Bishop Kelley suggested that he sell the creamery business. President Smith said, "We will not expect you to be self-sustaining, William."

Ruth watched her father, then fifty-four years old. "My wife and I have agreed that when we do this, it will be a real contribution to the good of the church, and if we do our part God will provide," he said. "Our older children are grown and can be left here. Our youngest daughter is almost seven; she will go with us."

Ruth was filled with excitement. She was going to visit the homeland of her parents. She would see where they had lived as children. She began to practice speaking and singing in the Welsh language.

The Saints in St. Joseph gave a farewell party. The creamery and household furniture were sold. The Lewises traveled to New York City where they were joined by Elder Frank J. Pierce, who was also going to serve as a missionary in Wales.

They left on November 2, 1901. That night a severe storm started and lasted several days. Waves were mountain high and tossed their ship about like a toy ball. Ruth and her mother were extremely sick. Many people on the ship feared it would sink.

During the last night of the storm, Ruth's father had a dream in which he saw the liner landing safely in Liverpool. In the dream he also saw Brother and Sister Thomas Gould with whom he and his family were to stay in Cardiff. This dream assured Brother Lewis that they would land safely.

During the storm Brother Lewis wrote the hymn, "One Hour with Jesus," which is in *The Hymnal*. Thousands of people have appreciated it, but to Ruth it has an even deeper, richer meaning.

When the ship landed in Liverpool, Apostle Gomer T. Griffiths was there to meet them. Brother and Sister Gould met them in the Union Station in Cardiff, South Wales. They were dressed exactly as Brother Lewis had seen them in the dream.

During the two years the Lewises spent in Wales, Ruth attended a school for girls eight hours a day, five days a week. At home she learned to knit, crochet, and sing.

Every Sunday evening after church services the Saints would meet at a home for a light lunch and a visit. The Welsh people are very hospitable, and Ruth enjoyed their association.

In July of 1903 the Lewis family returned to St. Joseph. Ruth started to school, and because she spoke with a Welsh accent, people often referred to her as "the little Welsh girl."

From then on for many years her father served as a church missionary. Because Sister Lewis and Ruth went with him, Ruth attended various schools. After graduation she took a secretarial course at Lackawana Business College in Scranton, Pennsylvania. About the time she finished her father was asked to go to the British Isles again as a missionary. Ruth and her mother accompanied him. While they were in England, Ruth became quite ill. Because of this, she and her mother returned to St. Joseph. Six months later, Brother Lewis also returned. When Ruth's health improved, she put her business training to use by doing stenographic work in local offices.

In 1910 her father was asked to serve as the patriarch of the Far West District, and the family moved to Cameron, Missouri. Here Ruth served as conference secretary when Far West District was made the Far West Stake. She was secretary of the Far West Religio, a general church organization for young people.

When her father gave a patriarchal blessing, she would take it in shorthand and then type it on a special form. She served as her father's secretary in Iowa, Kansas, Illinois, Ohio, Pennsylvania, New York, West Virginia, Saskatchewan, Alberta, and Manitoba. She also transcribed blessings for other patriarchs. Records show that she has recorded over two thousand.

While in Canada she experienced a wonderful healing that proved to her the importance of the work she was doing. At a district conference many people wanted their blessings. On the second day of the conference Ruth developed blood poisoning caused by using a pin to pick a splinter out of her finger. At first a large lump appeared near her elbow; then other lumps formed on her arm. The local doctor said she must go to the hospital immediately for an operation. She asked for administration. Following this she and another young woman went to a nearby home to try to get some rest. "Please, dear God, take charge," Ruth prayed. "For the benefit of the Saints who have traveled hundreds of miles for a blessing, please rebuke this disease and make me well." As she watched, the swelling went out of the hand and arm. The discoloration disappeared, and she realized she was miraculously healed. She returned to her father and was able to record over forty blessings for him that very day.

She was seventeen when she met Belle Robinson James. It was then that Sister James asked her to assist in reporting the business of the World Conferences of the church being held in Lamoni, Iowa. For the next eight years she assisted with conference minutes. "It was always a pleasant experience, and I learned much from her," Ruth wrote about Sister James.

For two years Ruth Lewis attended Missouri Wesleyan College in Cameron, Missouri, majoring in voice. She also took a correspondence course from the American School of Music in Chicago and studied under private teachers. Her understanding and appreciation of music has continued throughout the years.

In the summer of 1915 she was to serve as her father's secretary at the Brush Creek Reunion being held several miles from Xenia, Illinois. When they got off the train a young man—Mark Holman—came to them. He took them to the drugstore in Xenia which was owned by his aunt, Mrs. Mary Gauger, to await their ride to the reunion grounds. When the man came to take them and their luggage he had room only for Patriarch Lewis.

Ruth had to remain in Xenia and go with Mark the following day. A room was secured for her in the Xenia Hotel, and Mark took her to dinner. The next day they drove by horse and buggy to the reunion grounds. Ruth found a lot of work awaiting her there. She immediately became busy recording blessings and assisting with the music, but almost every evening after working in the drugstore, Mark Holman drove to the reunion to be with her. At first Ruth thought her life was too busy for romance. Then she had a dream that helped her realize Mark should become part of her life.

On Valentine's Day in 1918 they were married. They established their home in Xenia.

Although she worked six days a week in the store, Ruth continued to serve the church. For ten years she was music director of the Southeast Illinois District and for several years she was secretary of the Southeast Illinois District Sunday School.

Her father died March 29, 1919, and her mother November 8, 1921. Then in 1928 Ruth and Mark moved to Independence, Missouri, where both were active in church and community work. Their daughter, Margaret Ann, was born there.

Ruth's love of music brought her many close friends. She was a member of the Messiah Chorus, the Aeolian Chorus, the Gresty Quartet, the Stone Church Ladies Quartet, and the Stone Church Choir. For fifty-two consecutive Sundays she was a member of the double quartet that sang on Radio Station KMBC. During the forty years she was a member of the Independence Music Club she served in various offices. In 1951 she was made trustee (secretary) of the Nina G. Smith

Memorial Loan Fund of the Independence Music Club.

Ruth often wrote for church publications. One outstanding literary contribution she made was a series of biographies for the *Herald*. She also gave extensively of her time to the Blue Bird (Skylark) and Oriole programs. She was supervisor of the Blue Bird program for Center Stake and later became Blue Bird leader for the World Church. She corresponded with women and girls in many countries. For twenty-four years she served on the Girls Headquarters Committee (later this committee became known as the Girls Advisory Council). And for years she served as historian for the Center Stake Skylark and Oriole Administrative Council.

No task seemed too tedious or large for her if it had to do with the girls of the church. The Skylarks wore an overseas-type cap of blue with white piping. In order for girls in all parts of the world to wear the Skylark uniform she made almost five hundred of these caps.

In the summer of 1969 a luncheon was held in Independence in honor of Ruth Holman. President W. Wallace Smith was present for it. Edna Easter, who at one time was the director of girls work for the World Church, spoke on "The Five Lives of Ruth Holman." She said, "During the thirty-some years of church activities that Ruth and I have worked together, she has always been an example of true Christian living. She never draws attention to herself, but is always concerned about helping others."

MABEL

CARLILE

HYDE

Mabel Carlile always listened with interest when her mother and father told about their parents and grandparents in the early days of the church. Some of them had helped to build Kirtland Temple; some had suffered at Haun's Mill when the mob attacked there; some had crossed the frozen Mississippi when the Saints were fleeing from Missouri into Illinois; and some had moved with other Saints to Iowa.

Born February 5, 1896, in Underwood, Iowa, she moved with the family to Lamoni, Iowa, before she was old enough to go to school. Here she was baptized at the age of eight by J. A. Gunsolley. The influence of the church was constantly felt in the Carlile home. There was daily prayer, and both parents faithfully attended the local congregation. And always there was music. Her mother saw that Mabel had the opportunity to take piano lessons, and even as a young girl Mabel would say, "When I grow up I want to teach music at Graceland."

She completed grade school and high school in Lamoni and had hopes of attending Graceland, but because of family financial reverses she was unable to do so at that time. However, she did what she could to earn money for college. These earnings were supplemented by her mother who gave art lessons and painted pictures and china for sale. She was aided in still another way. A teacher, Lydia Wight, suggested a plan for getting sufficient college credits to teach music and art. Mabel took the state examination which at that time was required for any person who wanted to become a public school teacher. After receiving her certificate she taught in Lamoni and Lamont, Iowa.

Every summer during the years that she was teaching, she continued her own education, attending Graceland, Iowa State Teachers' College, and Des Moines University. From Northwestern University at Chicago, Illinois, she received both her bachelor's and master's degrees in music education. She was a member of Pi Lambda Theta, national honorary educational sorority.

In the midst of her struggle for an education, she had a serious accident that caused her to spend much time in the hospital. The money she had earned and had planned to use for her education had to be used for medical bills.

Fisher Carlile, her brother, wrote, "I could tell many

things of interest about Sis, but the one thing that stands out above all her service to humanity and free giving of her talents is her singing at nearly every funeral in Lamoni. In those horse-and-buggy days she would go out in that rainy, wet, cold Iowa weather whenever asked and use her rich soprano voice to help make a sorrowful experience a little beautiful."

In 1921 her dream of teaching at Graceland came true. President G. N. Briggs asked her to establish a Department of Music at the college and to teach there. Previous to this time, private lessons had been given at the college, but music had never been placed on a college credit basis and state certificates had not been granted enabling music students to teach in public schools.

In his book *Through the West Door,* Dr. Roy A. Cheville writes about Sister Carlile:

Courses were organized into a public school music curriculum and were designed to permit transfer to accredited schools. This gave a new push to both theoretical and applied music. Music organizations went through a transition. In 1923 choir and glee clubs were merged into an oratorio society. She directed the Department of Music from 1921 to 1945. Her insistence on thoroughness, academic standing, and appreciation of the standard of music has carried far beyond the boundaries of the campus. To sing a Christmas service of music, a dramatic oratorio, or a Russian anthem under her direction was a valued part of college life.

She received remunerative offers to teach at other colleges but refused. She says, "I never regarded teaching at Graceland as a sacrifice. How could I when I was doing the thing I loved and wanted to do? I was associated with fine men and women to whom teaching at Graceland was not a position but a stewardship."

"The time came during the depression when paychecks seldom came and then not for full amounts. However, a dedicated faculty kept on teaching and should be credited with keeping the doors of the beloved institution open," she wrote to a friend.

Under her guidance a three-year curriculum in music was organized. She founded and directed the A Cappella Choir in 1924 when this type of choral music was almost unknown in the Midwest. This group appeared in many cities and at various conventions. One hundred and fifty students were members of the Lamoni-Graceland Oratorio Society which she also founded.

After hearing one of her concerts a news reporter wrote, "There is a sincere quality about her that endears her to those with whom she comes in contact." Mabel Carlile believed that "people sing because they are inspired and are taught to sing, not because they are teased and scolded."

For a number of years she was president of the Iowa State Junior College Music Teachers Association. Under her guidance, music contests were held which included choral, small ensemble, and solo work. At several World Conferences she worked on the special music needed. She served as cochairman of the General Church Music Department with Paul N. Craig. Since both were full-time teachers they eventually succeeded in convincing church authorities that a general director of music should be appointed by the church. Franklyn Weddle, a former Carlile student, was selected.

The year 1943 brought another change into Mabel's

life. She married her next-door neighbor, Charles L. Hyde, a Lamoni businessman. Brother Hyde, a widower, had three daughters. Shortly after her marriage, Mabel left her teaching position at Graceland and remained home to care for Brother Hyde's mother, her own parents, and the youngest daughter who was ten years old. Years later she wrote, "These three daughters gave me some of the finest hours in my life."

In the fall of 1956 Sister Hyde returned to teach part time at Graceland as the instructor in a course in music literature and as director of the Chapel Choir. Of her return she said, "I have a firm conviction of the mission of Graceland in the life of the church. Recent spiritual experiences have given me a deep sense of stewardship." She continued this part-time assignment for five years. Upon retiring she was granted a professor emeritus standing at Graceland.

She has served on several committees for the World Church, including the committee which prepared the *Saints' Hymnal,* the committee which prepared *The Hymnal,* and the Advisory Music Committee.

Besides her many accomplishments in the field of music, she has served on the General Council of Women. She is an able student of the Book of Mormon and has taught classes on it to both young people and adults. Like her mother, she enjoys painting and has taught classes in art.

Today she lives in Lamoni among her many friends, but she has other friends throughout the world. They remember her because she established music not only at Graceland but also in their homes and in their hearts.

BIBLIOGRAPHY

Background material, references, and quotations were taken from the following sources: *Story of the Church* by Inez Smith Davis, *Ancestry and Posterity of Joseph Smith* by Audentia Anderson; *Biographical Sketches of Joseph Smith; Autumn Leaves; Thirty-three Women of the Restoration* by Emma Phillips; *Zion's Ensign; History of the Reorganized Church of Jesus Christ of Latter Day Saints;* Doctrine and Covenants; *Saints' Herald;* the files of Warren Van Dine; *University Bulletin; Kansas City Star; Black Cargoes* by Daniel P. Mannis; *Decisive Battles of the Civil War* by Joseph B. Mitchell; *The Strange Career of Jim Crow* by C. Vann Woodward; *Life Magazine; Slavery in America* by Marnett Hollander; *Strength to Love* by Martin Luther King, Jr.; *Joseph Smith III* by Audentia Anderson and Bertha Hulmes; *Stories of the Restoration;* ordination certificate of Ephrim Booker; letters from Gladys Robinson, Henrietta Booker, and Peggy Michael; Autobiography of C. Oscar Johnson (unpublished manuscript), Biography of Anna Johansson (manuscript) by James Everett; letter written by Mrs. Wayne Hewes; files of the Department of Statistics; History of Stone Church (manuscript) by Jay E. Keck; Autobiography of Emma Hougas (manuscript); Gamet Genealogy (manuscript); *Sunday School Exponent;* Conference Minutes; letters written by Ward A. Hougas; Beaucamper Cemetery markers; *Journal of History; On Memory's Beam* by Elbert A. Smith; *Stepping Stones; Building the Canadian Nation* by George W. Brown; *Restoration Witness;* Autobiography of Lottie Clark Diggle (manuscript);

interviews with A. B. Taylor and Marvin L. Diggle; *Into the Latter Day Light* by J. J. Cornish; letter from Opal Price; Alma Brookover manuscripts; Autobiography of E. M. Wildermuth (manuscript); personal files of Richard and Ruth Wildermuth; letters from Ava E. Wildermuth; *Conference Daily Herald; Adventures of a South Sea Missionary* by F. Edward Butterworth; interviews with Gladys Tyree, Madge Siegfried, Terii Maru, and Emere Mervin; personal files of Kathryn Westwood; letters from and interview with Adah Webb; conversations with Louise Jennings, Pauline Arnson, and Evelyn Velt; History of Englewood Congregation (manuscript); letter from Belle James; Biography of Alice Lewis (manuscript) by Floyd Potter; Biography of Alice Lewis (manuscript) by Alice Ley; "Report on Australia" by Gladys Grygo; "Report on Australia" by Gwen Roberts; interviews with Edith Lewis; Biography of Jessie Ward LeBaron (manuscript) by Melva L. Crum; *Through the West Door* by Roy A. Cheville; tape recording made by the family of Mabel Sanford Atkinson; interview with J. T. Westwood, Jr.; interviews with Herbert Lively and Jennie Z. Elliott; letter from Norma Smith; "Personally Yours" manuscript; *The Whole Wide World;* talk given at Business and Professional Women's meeting at Stone Church; *Temple Builders' Manual; Center Stake News;* address by Edna Easter; letter by Reed Holmes; letter by Carlile Fisher; and *Graceland College Alumni Magazine*

(Exact documentation available from author)

211